BEET,
Bastian's Early Blood Turnip.

RADISH,
Early Round Deep Scarlet.

TURNIP, D.M.F.& Co's.
Improved Purple Top Strap Leaved.

LETTUCE
Ferry's Early Priz

THE BEEKMAN 1802

HEIRLOOM VEGETABLE

COOKBOOK

CABBAGE.
Co's, Premium Flat Dutch.

WATER MELON.
D. M. FERRY & Co's Peerless.

SQUASH,
Hubbard.

MUSK-MELON,
Surprise

BRENT RIDGE AND
JOSH KILMER-PURCELL
AND **SANDY GLUCK**

THE BEEKMAN 1802

HEIRLOOM
VEGETABLE
COOKBOOK

100 DELICIOUS
HERITAGE RECIPES FROM THE
FARM AND GARDEN

RODALE

PHOTOGRAPHY BY **PAULETTE TAVORMINA**

© 2014 by Beekman 1802, LLC
Photographs © 2014 by Paulette Tavormina

Rodale books may be purchased for business or promotional use or for special sales. For information, please write to: Special Markets Department, Rodale Inc., 733 Third Avenue, New York, NY 10017

Printed in the United States of America
Rodale Inc. makes every effort to use acid-free ♾, recycled paper ♻.

Photographs by Paulette Tavormina except for pages 4, 8, 9, 14, 15, 24, 25, 34, 35, 38, 40–41, 47, 56–57, 72, 84–85, 89, 100, 110–111, 116–117, 120–121, 126–127, 138, 142–143, 150–151, 156, 170–171, 174–175, 200–201, 210, 252, 260–261, 265, and 276

Photograph of Brent Ridge, page 192, by Johannes Worsøe Berg

Book design by Amy C. King
Food styling by Paul Grimes
Prop styling by Cindy DiPrima

Library of Congress Cataloging-in-Publication Data

ISBN 978-1-60961-575-8 hardcover

Distributed to the trade by Macmillan

2 4 6 8 10 9 7 5 3 1 hardcover

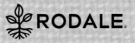

We inspire and enable people to improve their lives and the world around them.

rodalebooks.com

FOR ALL THOSE WHO CONTINUE TO GROW

Contents

Introduction

"No occupation is so delightful to me as the culture of the earth, and no culture comparable to that of the garden."

—THOMAS JEFFERSON

One warm summer day, a family with a 4-year-old came to visit us at Beekman Farm.

As we walked around the heirloom vegetable garden—52 raised beds on a half-acre plot in the heart of the farm, the child was fascinated by pulling carrots out of the ground, biting into a sugary pea pod, and plucking nasturtium blossoms and popping them into his mouth.

The boy's father commented, "I can't believe this! We can never get him to eat vegetables at home." Overhearing, the child looked up with his two fists full of salad greens and said, "These are vegetables?"

As the follow-up to the bestselling *The Beekman 1802 Heirloom Cookbook* and *The Beekman 1802 Heirloom Dessert Cookbook,* we wanted to create a book that would help people make the most of each season and provide recipes that make each vegetable taste like something so special that the 4-year-old in all of us would be impressed.

Like most home cooks, we start our meals by looking in the refrigerator, the pantry, and the cabinets (and the garden) for what ingredients we have on hand. The recipes in this book are meant for everyday use—dishes you'll likely be able to make from the items you have on hand or have found fresh in the market—with results so delicious that you won't even mind making them over and over again. Our goal is for you to use them so often that you'll know them like the back of your hand and won't even need the page as a reference.

As is the trademark of the other books in our Heirloom series, each recipe is accompanied by space for you to make notes and adaptations, and each seasonal section includes pages for you to include your family's own favorite meals. After all, it's your contributions that ultimately transform our collection of pretty paper into an heirloom for your own family.

"Eat all of your vegetables, or you can't have dessert."

How many of us heard this when growing up? Vegetables, for some reason, have often required the hard-sell approach. In creating *The Beekman 1802 Heirloom Vegetable Cookbook*, we were influenced by the gardening catalogs that fill our mailbox in January and February—well-timed for when winter has left the landscape of the farm its bleakest. For hundreds of years, America's seed houses have utilized nearly every marketing tool ever created to inspire a love affair with their little illustrated packets of hope. Their saturated images create fantasies of voluptuous produce and exceptional harvests. But they also promise that all of us can become farmers of something and that self-sufficiency can be both beautiful and delicious.

> *If this unpretending pamphlet should aid, even in a humble way, to advance the interest of agriculture, or contribute to the enjoyments of rural life, the object of our ambition will have been fully accomplished, and our efforts stimulated to renewed exertion.*
>
> —DAVID LANDRETH, 1848,
> FOUNDER OF D. LANDRETH SEED
> COMPANY, THE OLDEST SEED HOUSE
> IN AMERICA

RED CLUSTER PEPPER.

This is one of the most distinct and beautiful varieties we ever saw—in fact, the plants are so ornamental as to command a prominent position in the flower garden. The illustration shows the habit of growth; the leaves and berries. The small, thin peppers, of a deep scarlet-red color, are curiously massed together near the top of each branch. A single plant will exhibit of the handsome little peppers, which are abundant and prolific in flavor. The past season, Miss Ida Raney, Florence, Ky., sent us *two equal acres* or counted *twelve hundred and fifty-five peppers*, for which Cash Prizes of $25 and $10 for the plant, from one seed this year, that bears the greatest of peppers.

Per pkt., 10 cts.; 3 for 25 cts.; ½ ℔ $1.25; per ℔ $4.00.

NEW EARLY HACKENSACK MELON.

NEW EARLY HACKENSACK MELON.

This new strain, first sent out last year, was so highly recommended to us that we planted together and are pleased to endorse the claims made for it. By careful selection and improvement, carried on for some years, this strain has been so developed that it produces melons with all the good qualities of the well-known Hackensack Melon, but at least ten days earlier. A melon grower, near Albany, N. Y., states that with him the New Early Hackensack was at least two weeks earlier than the Old Hackensack; and that with these thirty-five early melons in a barrel, he had no difficulty in selling his crop in the Albany markets for $1.00 per barrel. The melons weigh from four to ten pounds each, are of a oblong shape, heavily netted, and have light-green flesh of delicious flavor.

Per pkt. 10 cts.; oz. 20 cts.; ¼ ℔ 60 cts.; per ℔ $2.00.

CROPP'S GIANT PEPPER.

Silas Fulmer, South Bend, Pa., Sept. 23d, 1887, writes:—The seeds I purchased of you last season proved to be first class. The Green Fern Cucumber exceeded the Turner Hybrid Tomato. The Scotland Cabbage beats them all. My neighbors are surprised to see the great things of all. My neighbors came in, dry season, and I tell them if they would buy their seed of W. Atlee Burpee & Co., they would have just such a melon challenge the same as I did. I think it well they could raise, Morning Green Nutmeg Muskmelon. I also had some choice beans of you last spring. Muskmelons from seed I pur...

WESTERFIELD'S CHICAGO PICKLE.

WESTERFIELD'S NEW IMPROVED CHICAGO PICKLE CUCUMBER.

Of late years Chicago has taken a prominent position in the manufacture of pickles, and necessarily the growers have tried to secure the most profitable varieties. Mr. Westerfield, who has been interested largely in the business, claims that in this very prolific variety he has combined all the qualities desired by those who raise cucumbers for commercial pickles, and he refers to nearly every large factory in Chicago. Of the two we are not sure we are, previously, not yet prepared to say whether Nichols' or Westerfield's is the best, but we do know that both are good.

Per pkt. 10 cts.; oz. 25 cts.; ¼ ℔ 40 cts.; per ℔ $1.25.

ORDER DEPARTMENT.

SHIPPING OFFICE.

A STORE ROOM.

SEED POTATO STORES.

TOMATO
JOHN BAER
ORO GROSSO

...ARD SEED. CO.
FREDONIA, N.Y.

SQUASH
SUMMER

Spring

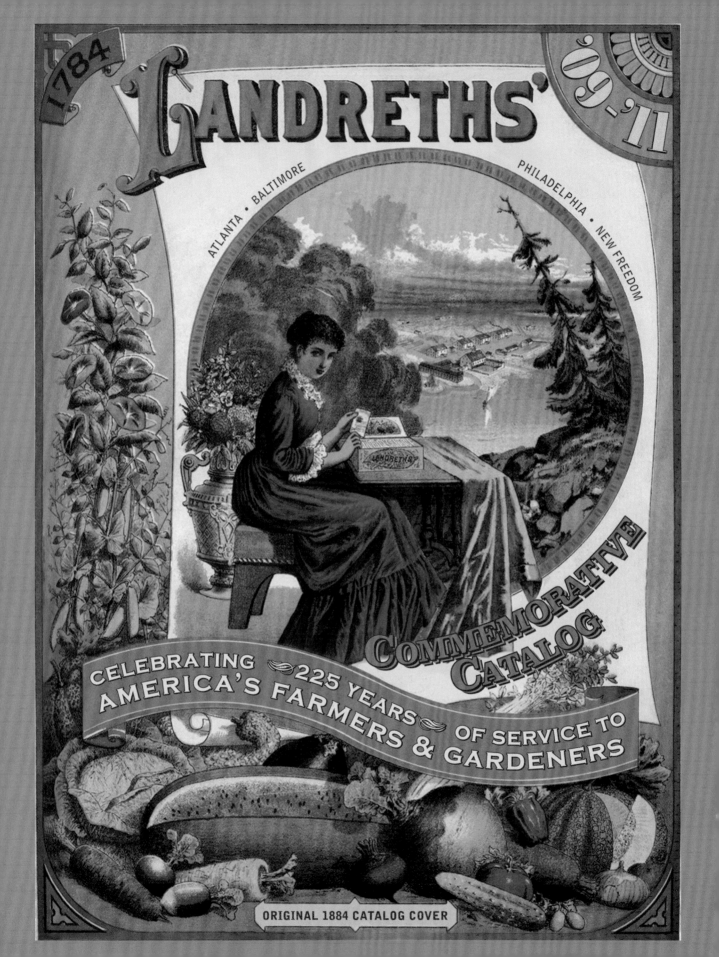

ATLANTA · BALTIMORE

PHILADELPHIA · NEW FREEDOM

1784

LANDRETHS'

'09-'11

COMMEMORATIVE CATALOG

CELEBRATING AMERICA'S 225 YEARS OF SERVICE TO FARMERS & GARDENERS

ORIGINAL 1884 CATALOG COVER

Spring

Spring Pea Soup *7*

Deep-Fried Baby Artichokes
with Roasted Pepper Sauce *10*

Green Herb Salad Dressing *12*

Creamy Young Greens Soup *13*

Pea Shoots Asian-Style with Garlic, Ginger,
and Sesame *17*

Radishes with Sorrel Butter *18*

Jerusalem Artichoke Pancakes *21*

Teacup Jello Salad with Arugula *22*

Radicchio and Endive Salad with Dried Cherries *27*

Asparagus and Prosciutto Wrapped in Puff Pastry *28*

Shrimp with Garlic Scapes *31*

Penne with Roasted Salmon, Asparagus, Peas,
and Ramps *32*

Feta Cheese with Arugula Pesto and Honey *33*

Fish Wrapped in Lettuce *36*

Fava Beans with Shaved Parmesan and Olive Oil *39*

Masala Chicken with Rhubarb *42*

Oven-Fried Crispy Spinach *45*

Chilled Radish Soup *46*

Leek Tangle *49*

A Trio of Horseradishes *52*

Rhubarb Soda Floats *54*

Baked Spinach Custards *55*

Assorted Dressings for Young Lettuce *58*

Fresh Mint Syrup *61*

Artichoke, Fava Bean, and Asparagus Stew *62*

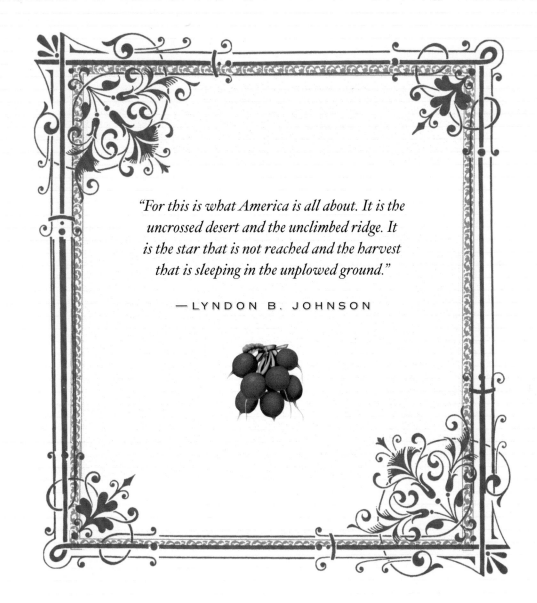

"For this is what America is all about. It is the uncrossed desert and the unclimbed ridge. It is the star that is not reached and the harvest that is sleeping in the unplowed ground."

—LYNDON B. JOHNSON

SPRING PEA SOUP

There's still a little chill in the air when the first peas are ready for picking. This soup is perfect in the spring when young lettuces are around.

2 tablespoons unsalted butter

2 leeks, thinly sliced and well washed

6 cups tender green lettuce leaves, well washed and dried

1/3 cup fresh mint leaves

2 cups shelled fresh green peas (see Tidbit)

3/4 teaspoon coarse (kosher) salt

1/2 teaspoon freshly ground black pepper

2 cups chicken or vegetable broth

1/3 cup heavy cream

2 teaspoons fresh lemon juice

TIDBIT: *To get 2 cups of shelled peas, you'll need to start with about 2 pounds of peas in the pod, so feel free to use frozen peas here (we'll never tell).*

In a large saucepan, melt the butter over medium-low heat. Add the leeks and cook, stirring occasionally, for 10 minutes, or until tender.

Add the lettuce and mint and cook for 5 minutes, stirring occasionally, until the lettuce is very tender.

Stir in the peas, salt, and pepper and stir to combine. Add the broth and bring to a boil. Reduce to a simmer, cover, and cook for 5 minutes, or until the peas are tender and the flavors have blended.

Working in 2 batches, transfer the soup to a blender and puree until smooth. Add the cream and lemon juice and blend. Serve hot.

Notes

DEEP-FRIED BABY ARTICHOKES WITH ROASTED PEPPER SAUCE

The saying goes that spring showers bring forth the flowers, and the last time we checked, this seemed to still be true. The artichoke is technically a flower bud that has not yet bloomed, so it's a perfect way to add a little bit of the tantalizing season to your plate. This sauce can easily be doubled or tripled and is great tossed with a bowl of pasta.

2 garlic cloves, peeled

1 large red bell pepper

¼ cup raw (skin-on) almonds

¼ cup extra-virgin olive oil

3 tablespoons water

2 tablespoons tomato paste

1½ teaspoons sweet smoked paprika

½ teaspoon coarse (kosher) salt

1 tablespoon plus 2 teaspoons fresh lemon juice

1 pound baby artichokes

Vegetable oil, for deep-frying

Preheat the broiler with the rack 4 inches from the heat source.

In a small saucepan of boiling water, cook the garlic for 2 minutes to blanch. Drain.

Cut the pepper vertically into flat panels. Place the panels, skin-side up, on a broiler pan and broil for 10 minutes, or until the skin is blackened. Transfer the peppers to a plate, skin-side down. When cool enough to handle, peel. Transfer to a food processor and add the blanched garlic, almonds, olive oil, water, tomato paste, smoked paprika, salt, and 2 teaspoons of the lemon juice, and puree.

Add the remaining 1 tablespoon lemon juice to a large bowl of cold water (this is "acidulated water"). Snap off the dark outer leaves of the artichokes until you're down to paler green leaves. Trim the very bottom of the stem and, with a paring knife, remove the outer layer of the stem. Cut about ½ inch off the tips of the artichoke leaves. Halve the artichokes lengthwise and place in the bowl of acidulated water to prevent them from discoloring.

In a deep saucepan, pour in the vegetable oil to come up 2 inches. Heat the oil over medium heat to 350°F on a deep-frying thermometer. (Alternatively, if you don't have a thermometer, drop a little flour into the oil; if it sizzles, the oil is ready.)

Lift the artichokes from the water and dry on paper towels. Working in batches, deep-fry the artichokes for 8 to 10 minutes, or until crispy. Drain on paper towels and serve the sauce on the side for dipping.

 Notes

GREEN HERB SALAD DRESSING

We like this tossed with soft buttery lettuce such as Boston. (And if no one is watching, we use it as a dip for potato chips!)

¼ cup fresh basil leaves

¼ cup fresh mint leaves

¼ cup fresh dill fronds

2 tablespoons snipped chives

2 tablespoons extra-virgin olive oil

⅓ cup buttermilk

2 tablespoons fresh lemon juice

½ teaspoon coarse (kosher) salt

In a food processor or blender, combine the basil, mint, dill, chives, and oil and pulse until finely chopped. Add the buttermilk, lemon juice, and salt and puree until smooth. Refrigerate until ready to use or for up to 1 week.

Notes —

CREAMY YOUNG GREENS SOUP

We grow or raise nearly all the food that we consume. You can imagine that by the first of spring, we are eager for anything green. While we've used escarole, kale, and beet greens, you can sometimes find bags of mixed baby greens in the market, and they would be perfect here. Use a total of 10 ounces for this mild, verdant soup, which gets its velvety texture from egg yolks.

3 tablespoons unsalted butter

2 baby leeks, halved lengthwise, thinly sliced crosswise, and well washed

2 garlic cloves, thinly sliced

2 cups thinly sliced baby escarole

2 cups thinly sliced baby kale

2 cups thinly sliced baby beet greens

$\frac{1}{2}$ teaspoon dried rosemary

4 cups chicken broth

$\frac{3}{4}$ teaspoon coarse (kosher) salt

2 large egg yolks

2 tablespoons fresh lemon juice

TIDBIT: *The process of adding some hot liquid to egg yolks to warm them before adding the egg yolks to a hot liquid is called tempering. The idea is to bring the egg yolks to the same temperature as the soup so that when you add them in, the soup will thicken smoothly instead of curdling the eggs.*

In a large saucepan, melt the butter over medium-low heat. Add the leeks and garlic and cook for 5 to 7 minutes, stirring occasionally, until the leeks are tender.

Add the escarole, kale, beet greens, and rosemary and cook for 7 to 10 minutes, stirring occasionally, until the greens are very tender. Add the broth and salt and bring to a boil. Reduce to a simmer and cook for 5 minutes to concentrate the flavors.

Working in batches, transfer the soup to a blender and puree until smooth. Return the soup to the saucepan.

In a medium bowl, whisk the egg yolks to break them up. Whisking constantly, gradually add about a cup of the hot soup to the egg yolks (see Tidbit). Bring the soup to a simmer, then whisk in the egg yolk mixture and cook for 1 minute over low heat until thickened. Stir in the lemon juice and serve hot.

Notes _____

_____

_____

PEA SHOOTS ASIAN-STYLE WITH GARLIC, GINGER, AND SESAME

Look for thin, tender pea shoots (they actually taste like peas) in farmers' markets, or, if you can't find them, use a bunch of watercress instead.

2 teaspoons sesame seeds

2 tablespoons vegetable oil

2 tablespoons sliced fresh ginger

3 garlic cloves, peeled and halved

3 tablespoons water

2 scallions, thinly sliced

¼ pound pea shoots, well washed and dried

¼ teaspoon coarse (kosher) salt

2 teaspoons toasted sesame oil

TIDBIT: *The only reason peas are green is that they are picked when still immature. A ripe pea is actually more yellow in color. Eating green peas became fashionable in the 1600s and 1700s but was described by the French as "madness." Up until then, only pea shoots were considered digestible.*

In a small dry skillet, toast the sesame seeds over low heat for 1 minute, tossing frequently, until fragrant. Transfer to a plate.

In a large skillet, heat the vegetable oil over low heat. Add the ginger, garlic, and water. Cover and cook for 7 to 10 minutes, stirring once or twice, until the ginger and garlic are very tender. Leaving the liquid in the pan, discard the ginger and garlic.

Add the scallions and pea shoots to the pan, sprinkle with the salt, and cook for 2 minutes, or until the pea shoots are tender. Transfer to a platter, drizzle with the sesame oil, and scatter the toasted sesame seeds over the top.

Notes

RADISHES WITH SORREL BUTTER

Radishes split down the middle and stuffed with salted butter was our most memorable culinary delight from the first vacation we took together to the south of France. Sorrel is around in the spring and has a tart, lemony taste (although it can vary from mild to very tart).

8 tablespoons (1 stick) unsalted
   butter, at room temperature

2 tablespoons minced shallot

1 cup packed sorrel leaves, coarsely
   chopped

2 teaspoons fresh lemon juice

¼ teaspoon coarse (kosher) salt

2 bunches radishes

In a large skillet, melt 1 tablespoon of the butter over low heat. Add the shallot and cook for 2 to 3 minutes, or until tender. Add the sorrel and cook for 3 to 4 minutes, or until the sorrel is very tender. Transfer to a bowl and let cool to room temperature.

Add the remaining 7 tablespoons room-temperature butter to the sorrel mixture along with the lemon juice and salt. Mash to combine.

Arrange the radishes in a bowl and serve the sorrel butter on the side.

Notes

JERUSALEM ARTICHOKE PANCAKES

Jerusalem artichokes are one of the few vegetables that are native to the North American plains. And although they're available year-round, we find them sweeter in the spring, right after a light frost. The plants were first described in 1805 after Indians living in the Dakotas served them to Lewis and Clark. Once you've made the pancakes, try the Jerusalem artichokes roasted with herbs and olive oil just like potatoes. Serve the pancakes for an appetizer or as a side dish to accompany a lemony roast chicken.

1 pound Jerusalem artichokes, well scrubbed and dried

1 small onion, peeled

2 tablespoons all-purpose flour

1 large egg

3/4 teaspoon coarse (kosher) salt

1/4 teaspoon freshly ground black pepper

4 tablespoons olive oil

Sour cream, for serving

TIDBIT: *Not related to the artichoke at all, the name is thought to be derived from a mispronunciation of the Italian word for sunflower, girasole. The blossoms of the tuber resemble a sunflower. P.S. Jerusalem artichokes contain inulin, a type of carbohydrate that some people can't digest, which can cause bloating and digestive issues.*

On the large holes of a grater, grate the Jerusalem artichokes and the onion into a large bowl. Add the flour, egg, salt, and pepper and mix to combine.

In a large skillet, heat 2 tablespoons of the oil over medium heat. Drop the mixture by 1/4-cup mounds, 4 at a time, into the pan and flatten with a spatula to a 1/2-inch thickness. Cook for 3 to 4 minutes per side, or until the pancakes are golden brown and cooked through. Repeat with the remaining 2 tablespoons oil and remaining Jerusalem artichoke mixture.

Serve 2 pancakes per person with a dollop of sour cream.

Notes ————————————————

TEACUP JELLO SALAD WITH ARUGULA

Arugula, also called salad rocket, was not cultivated in the United States until the 1970s and is one of the few vegetables we have that exists in its pure, unadulterated form. Here we put its peppery kick to good use. If you prefer, you can make this in an 8-cup bowl and serve it from the bowl.

½ cup pecans

2 envelopes (¼ ounce each) plain
    unflavored gelatin

¾ cup cold water

1½ cups fresh lime juice (about
    12 limes)

1½ cups sugar

½ cup heavy cream

½ cup whole-milk ricotta cheese

1 can (8 ounces) juice-packed
    crushed pineapple

⅓ cup finely diced celery

1 cup baby arugula, finely chopped

TIDBIT: *The long, slow toasting of the pecans ensures that they will remain crisp in the salad.*

Preheat the oven to 250°F. Place the pecans in a small pan and toast for 1 hour, or until crisp (see Tidbit). When cool enough to handle, coarsely chop.

In a glass measuring cup, sprinkle the gelatin over the cold water and let stand 5 minutes until swollen. In a small saucepan, bring 1 cup of the lime juice and the sugar to a simmer over low heat, stirring for 2 minutes until the sugar has dissolved. Stir in the gelatin and cook for 1 minute until melted.

Transfer the lime juice mixture to a bowl and stir in the remaining ½ cup lime juice. Refrigerate for 30 minutes until it's the consistency of honey.

In a large bowl, with an electric mixer, beat the cream until soft peaks form. On low speed, beat in the lime mixture. With a rubber spatula, fold in the pecans, ricotta, pineapple, celery, and arugula. Spoon into eight 6-ounce teacups or custard cups and refrigerate for 1 hour, or until set.

Notes _____

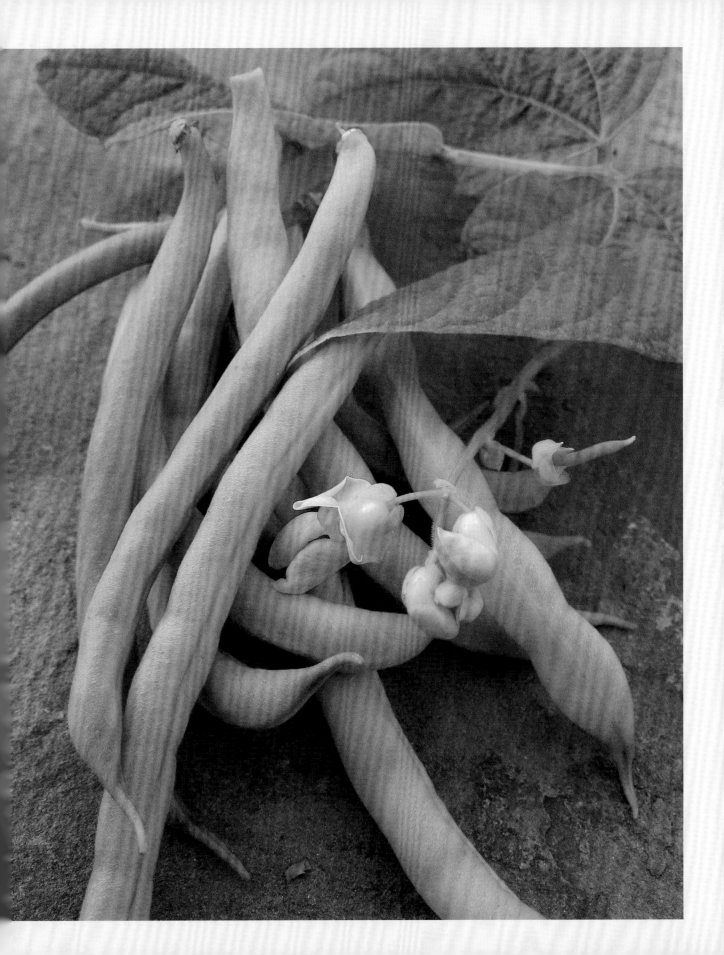

RADICCHIO AND ENDIVE SALAD WITH DRIED CHERRIES

Bitter radicchio, bittersweet Belgian endive, and dried cherries come together in a lightly sweetened vinaigrette to make a refreshing salad. The honey offsets the bitterness of the radicchio and endive, and the pumpkin seeds provide a bit of crunch.

1 tablespoon plus 1 teaspoon cider vinegar

1 tablespoon extra-virgin olive oil

1 teaspoon honey

1 teaspoon Dijon mustard

$\frac{1}{4}$ teaspoon coarse (kosher) salt

$\frac{1}{4}$ teaspoon freshly ground black pepper

2 Belgian endive (8 ounces total), halved lengthwise and sliced crosswise into $\frac{1}{2}$-inch pieces

1 radicchio (8 ounces), halved, cored, and cut into $\frac{1}{2}$-inch chunks

3 tablespoons dried cherries

1 tablespoon hulled pumpkin seeds

TIDBIT: *Radicchio and endive are both part of the chicory family. What Americans call endive, the British call chicory, and what the Americans call chicory, the British call endive.*

In a large bowl, whisk together the vinegar, oil, honey, mustard, salt, and pepper until thick. Add the endive, radicchio, cherries, and pumpkin seeds and toss to coat. Serve immediately.

Notes

ASPARAGUS AND PROSCIUTTO WRAPPED IN PUFF PASTRY

This is a classic hors d'oeuvre—an heirloom recipe for sure.

All-purpose flour, for the work surface

1 sheet (7 to 8 ounces) frozen all-butter puff pastry, thawed but still cold

2 tablespoons Dijon mustard

2 teaspoons fresh lemon juice

½ teaspoon crumbled dried rosemary

4 ounces thinly sliced prosciutto, cut into 16 long pieces

16 thick asparagus spears (about 1 pound), ends trimmed

TIDBIT: *Choose bright green asparagus stalks with purple-tinged tips. Look for stalks that have a smooth skin, that are uniform in color, and have a dry, compact tip. Avoid wilted or limp stalks. Shriveled stalks are a sign of age. To store asparagus, wrap the stem ends in damp paper towels for several days. To extend the life, refrigerate stalks, tips up, in a glass with a small amount of water.*

Preheat the oven to 400°F. Line a baking sheet with parchment paper.

On a lightly floured work surface, roll the puff pastry to a 10 × 12-inch rectangle. In a small bowl, stir together the mustard, lemon juice, and rosemary and brush the mixture over the pastry. Cut the dough crosswise into sixteen 10-inch-long strips.

Spiral wrap the prosciutto around the asparagus from end to tip. Spiral wrap the puff pastry around the prosciutto, mustard-side in. Place the asparagus on the baking sheet and bake for 20 minutes, or until the pastry is crisp and golden.

Notes ——————————————————

SHRIMP WITH GARLIC SCAPES

We've used garlic scapes—the edible, curling stalks of the garlic plant—for our take on shrimp scampi. Snipped from the garden while still tender, scapes provide mild garlicky goodness with an asparagus-like texture.

1 tablespoon plus 1 teaspoon olive oil

5 garlic scapes, thinly sliced (½ cup)

1 pound large shrimp, peeled and deveined

½ pound sugar snap peas, strings removed

½ teaspoon coarse (kosher) salt

1 teaspoon grated lemon zest

3 tablespoons fresh lemon juice

2 tablespoons chopped fresh flat-leaf parsley

2 tablespoons cold unsalted butter, cut up

TIDBIT: *The scapes must be trimmed off the garlic plant in order for the garlic bulb growing beneath the soil to reach its full potential. Otherwise the plant is using energy to flower and reproduce rather than growing the bulb.*

In a large skillet, heat the oil over medium-low heat. Add the garlic scapes and cook for 5 minutes, stirring occasionally, until tender.

Add the shrimp, sugar snaps, salt, and lemon zest and cook for 5 minutes, stirring occasionally, until the shrimp are just cooked through. Stir in the lemon juice and parsley, remove the pan from the heat, and swirl in the butter until creamy.

Notes

PENNE WITH ROASTED SALMON, ASPARAGUS, PEAS, AND RAMPS

In upstate New York, ramps are a religion, and people closely guard the location of the patches—usually hidden in a wooded area. Ramps are a wild member of the onion family and are around in the early spring. If you can't find them, use scallions instead. Mayonnaise, that kitchen standby, is the foundation of a creamy sauce. We find thick asparagus sweeter than the thinner variety, but choose your favorite.

8 ounces penne, ziti, or any short tubular pasta

1 pound asparagus spears, preferably thick, ends trimmed, spears cut into 2-inch lengths

1 cup shelled fresh or unthawed frozen green peas

1 pound skin-on salmon fillet, in one piece

1 teaspoon coarse (kosher) salt

6 ramps or scallions, cut into 2-inch lengths

3 tablespoons fresh lemon juice

3 tablespoons mayonnaise

2 tablespoons extra-virgin olive oil

1 teaspoon finely chopped fresh tarragon leaves or 1/2 teaspoon dried

Preheat the oven to 450°F.

In a large pot of boiling water, cook the pasta according to package directions, adding the asparagus during the final 2 minutes of cooking and the peas during the last 1 minute. Drain well.

Meanwhile, place the salmon skin-side down on a rimmed baking sheet, sprinkle with ¼ teaspoon of the salt, and scatter the ramps around. Roast for 10 minutes, or until the salmon is just cooked through and the ramps are tender.

In a large bowl, whisk together the lemon juice, mayonnaise, oil, tarragon, and the remaining ¾ teaspoon salt. Add the hot pasta and vegetables and the roasted ramps and toss to combine.

To serve, transfer the pasta mixture to a serving platter and break the salmon pieces over the top.

 Notes _____

FETA CHEESE WITH ARUGULA PESTO AND HONEY

People think pesto can only be made from basil and pine nuts, but we've made pesto from nasturtium leaves and walnuts, mint leaves, and even garlic scapes. Here we use arugula. Store this pesto in the fridge for up to 3 days or freeze for longer storage. It's good spooned over soft goat cheese as well.

1 large garlic clove, peeled

2 cups arugula leaves (2 ounces)

3 tablespoons extra-virgin olive oil

2 tablespoons toasted pine nuts

1 tablespoon fresh lemon juice

½ teaspoon coarse (kosher) salt

1 pound feta cheese, cut into
   8 slices

¼ cup honey

In a small pot of boiling water, cook the garlic for 2 minutes to blanch. With a slotted spoon, transfer the garlic to a plate but leave the water boiling. Add the arugula leaves to the water and cook for 10 seconds to set their color. Drain, rinse under cold water, and squeeze dry.

In a food processor, combine the arugula, garlic, oil, pine nuts, lemon juice, and salt and puree until smooth.

Divide the feta among 8 plates, drizzle each with 1½ teaspoons of the honey, and top each with 1 tablespoon of the arugula pesto.

Notes

FISH WRAPPED IN LETTUCE

When we make this recipe, we go down to the pond on the farm and catch a largemouth bass. For easier sourcing, we've used striped bass here, but really any mild fish would work well. A simple wrap of lettuce keeps the fish super moist; and the butter, herbs, and wine make an easy pan sauce.

6 tablespoons unsalted butter, at room temperature

½ teaspoon coarse (kosher) salt

1 teaspoon grated lemon zest

1 teaspoon fresh lemon juice

1 tablespoon chopped fresh flat-leaf parsley

1 tablespoon snipped fresh dill

8 large, soft lettuce leaves (such as Boston)

4 skinless striped bass fillets (6 ounces each)

½ cup white wine

Preheat the oven to 350°F.

In a small bowl, mash the butter with the salt, lemon zest, lemon juice, parsley, and dill.

Place 4 lettuce leaves on a work counter and top each with a fillet. Top each fillet with the butter mixture, dividing it equally among the fillets. Add another leaf and wrap them around each other to enclose the fish.

Place the wrapped fish in a 9 × 9-inch baking dish and pour the wine on top. Cover with foil and bake for 20 minutes, or until the fish can be pierced with a knife. (Timing may vary depending upon the thickness of the fillets.)

To serve, place the lettuce-wrapped fish on plates and spoon the pan juices on top.

Notes

FAVA BEANS WITH SHAVED PARMESAN AND OLIVE OIL

Preparing fava beans is a labor of love, as 2 pounds will yield just a little over 1 cup shelled favas. But it's well worth it. These beans are rich and meaty. Toss them with a full-flavored extra-virgin olive oil.

2 pounds fresh fava beans
   in the pod

1 tablespoon extra-virgin olive oil

$^1/_2$ teaspoon grated lemon zest

1 tablespoon fresh lemon juice

$^1/_2$ teaspoon coarse (kosher) salt

2 ounces Parmesan cheese, shaved
   with a vegetable peeler

Remove the fava beans from their pods and discard the pods.

In a large pot of boiling water, cook the beans for 1 minute. Drain. If the fava beans are very small, about the size of a pinky fingernail, you can leave them in their skins. If not, slip them out of their skins.

Transfer the beans to a large bowl. Add the oil, lemon zest, lemon juice, and salt and toss to coat. Serve with the Parmesan scattered over the top.

Notes

THE HEIRLOOM VEGETABLE GARDEN AT
THE BEEKMAN 1802 FARM

MASALA CHICKEN WITH RHUBARB

J osh makes red currant jelly from the fruit of currant bushes that have been growing on the farm for a long time. If you've got access to fresh currants, try making your own. There's no need to top or tail them; simply weigh the currants (stems and all) and use an equal amount of sugar. Stir them together in a saucepan and once it comes to a boil, cook for 8 minutes. Strain and that's it.

2¼ teaspoons coarse (kosher) salt

1½ teaspoons garam masala

1½ teaspoons sugar

¾ teaspoon ground ginger

½ teaspoon ground cardamom

¼ teaspoon freshly ground black pepper

8 bone-in, skin-on chicken thighs (3 pounds)

3 tablespoons olive oil

¼ cup all-purpose flour

3 garlic cloves, thinly sliced

¼ cup finely chopped shallots or red onion

1 cup chicken broth

¼ cup red currant jelly

2 tablespoons orange juice

2 tablespoons unsalted butter

¾ pound rhubarb, cut into 1-inch lengths

TIDBIT: *1 pound of fresh rhubarb yields about 3 cups chopped.*

Preheat the oven to 350°F.

In a large bowl, combine the salt, garam masala, sugar, ginger, cardamom, and pepper. Add the chicken and rub the spice mixture into the skin and under it as well.

In a large ovenproof skillet, heat the oil over medium heat. Dredge the chicken in the flour, shaking off any excess. Add the chicken to the skillet and cook for 2 to 3 minutes per side, or until browned. Transfer to a plate.

Add the garlic and shallots to the pan and cook for 2 minutes, stirring frequently. Add the broth, jelly, and orange juice and bring to a boil. Return the chicken to the pan, cover, and place in the oven. Bake for 30 to 35 minutes, or until the chicken is cooked through.

Meanwhile, in a large skillet, heat the butter over medium heat. Add the rhubarb and cook, stirring occasionally, or until tender but not mushy.

Stir the rhubarb into the pan juices and serve the chicken with the sauce and rhubarb spooned over.

Notes _____

_____

_____

OVEN-FRIED CRISPY SPINACH

Catherine de Medici was so enamored of spinach that she had one chef devoted exclusively to preparing it in her kitchen. Spinach Florentine originated at her table. Here's a Beekman 1802 use of spinach that requires very little culinary mastery. Easier than deep-frying, the spinach emerges from the oven crisp and sweet. Don't be alarmed by the amount of spinach called for in this recipe; it cooks down considerably and will go in a flash!

1 pound fresh spinach, stems discarded, leaves well washed and dried (about 16 cups spinach)

2 tablespoons olive oil

Coarse (kosher) salt

Position the racks in the upper and lower thirds of the oven and preheat to 425°F.

Divide the spinach between 2 large rimmed baking sheets, drizzle each with 1 tablespoon oil, then gently massage the oil into the leaves.

Roast for 15 to 17 minutes, switching the baking sheets from top to bottom midway through, until the spinach is crispy.

Sprinkle the crisp spinach with salt to taste, and serve hot or at room temperature.

Notes ————————————————————————

———————————————————————————————

———————————————————————————————

CHILLED RADISH SOUP

This is super refreshing. The tangy buttermilk, rich walnuts, and vinegar complement the peppery radishes. This is loosely based on a cold green bean soup that Sandy's mom, Frances Gluck, used to make.

½ pound radishes, thinly sliced

2 cups buttermilk

¼ cup walnuts or pecans

1 tablespoon red wine vinegar

½ teaspoon coarse (kosher) salt

½ teaspoon sugar

½ pound Yukon Gold potatoes

2 large eggs

¼ cup finely diced red onion

1 mini (aka Persian) cucumber, thinly sliced

TIDBIT: *There are five varieties of radishes: red globe (the most common), black, daikons, white icicles, and California Mammoth White.*

Place all but ¼ cup of the radishes in a blender along with the buttermilk, walnuts, vinegar, salt, and sugar and puree until smooth. Refrigerate until well chilled.

While the soup chills, place the potatoes in a small saucepan of salted water and bring to a boil. Reduce to a simmer and cook for 30 minutes, or until the potatoes are fork-tender but not falling apart. Run under cold water, peel, and cut into ½-inch chunks.

Place the eggs in a separate saucepan of water and bring to a boil over high heat. Remove from the heat, cover, and let stand 12 minutes. Crack the eggs, transfer to a bowl of ice water, and let stand 10 minutes (this makes peeling easier). Drain, peel, and thinly slice.

To serve, divide the soup among chilled bowls. Garnish with the potatoes, eggs, onion, cucumber, and the reserved radishes.

Notes _____

LEEK TANGLE

An easy spring side dish that pairs well with almost anything else you are likely serving. Sweet, mellow, and all tangled up.

4 leeks, tender green and white
    parts, quartered lengthwise

2 tablespoons sugar

1 tablespoon fresh lemon juice

3 tablespoons unsalted butter

1 teaspoon finely chopped fresh
    tarragon leaves

¾ teaspoon coarse (kosher) salt

TIDBIT: *Lemon juice added to the sugar when caramelizing prevents it from crystallizing and gives it a tangy edge.*

Place the leeks in a bowl of tepid water. Swish the leeks around, then let them sit so that any grit will settle to the bottom of the bowl. Scoop the leeks out with your hands without disturbing the water (so the grit remains in the bottom of the bowl). Repeat with fresh water until no grit remains.

In a medium saucepan of boiling water, cook the leeks for 5 minutes, or until tender. Drain and dry well.

In a small skillet, melt the sugar with the lemon juice (see Tidbit) over medium heat for 3 to 4 minutes, or until the sugar has lightly caramelized and is the color of a brown paper bag. Remove from the heat, swirl in the butter, tarragon, and salt until the butter has melted. Pour the mixture over the leeks and toss well.

Notes

A TRIO OF HORSERADISHES

Make a few batches of horseradish when the fresh root is in season. Fresh horseradish is incredibly pungent, so avert your face from the processor when pureeing (though it's great if you want to clear your nasal passages). Prepared horseradish will keep in a tightly closed container in the fridge for several months.

WHITE HORSERADISH

6 ounces peeled fresh horseradish
(from $1/2$ pound)

$1/3$ cup distilled white vinegar

1 tablespoon sugar

$1/4$ teaspoon coarse (kosher) salt

RED BEET HORSERADISH

6 ounces peeled fresh horseradish
(from $1/2$ pound)

1 small beet (4 ounces), peeled

$1/3$ cup distilled white vinegar

1 teaspoon sugar

$1/4$ teaspoon coarse (kosher) salt

YELLOW CURRY HORSERADISH

6 ounces peeled fresh horseradish
(from $1/2$ pound)

$1/3$ cup distilled white vinegar

1 tablespoon sugar

2 teaspoons curry powder

$1/4$ teaspoon salt

To make the white horseradish: In a food processor, with the grating disk, grate the horseradish. Add the vinegar, sugar, and salt and puree until smooth.

To make the red beet horseradish: In a food processor, with the grating disk, grate the horseradish and the beet. Add the vinegar, sugar, and salt and puree until smooth.

To make the yellow curry horseradish: In a food processor, with the grating disk, grate the horseradish. Add the vinegar, sugar, curry powder, and salt and puree until smooth.

TIDBIT: *Horseradish is still planted and harvested mostly by hand, making that 24 million pounds produced in America each year even more astounding. Bottled horseradish was sold commercially as early as 1860, making it one of the first condiments sold as a convenience food.*

Notes

RHUBARB SODA FLOATS

Don't pitch the cooked rhubarb, ginger, and orange zest. Serve it as you would applesauce or use it like jam.

1 cup sugar

1 cup water

1 pound rhubarb, thinly sliced

¼ cup thinly sliced fresh ginger
   (no need to peel)

4 strips orange zest
   (2 inches long x ½ inch wide)

Seltzer

Vanilla ice cream

TIDBIT: *Rhubarb became popular as a food in the 17th century when cheap sugar became available, thus making the vegetable's extreme tartness more palatable.*

In a medium saucepan, combine the sugar, water, rhubarb, ginger, and orange zest and bring to a boil over medium heat. Reduce to a simmer, cover, and cook for 15 minutes, or until the rhubarb is very tender.

Set a fine-mesh sieve over a bowl and drain the syrup into the bowl, pressing to extract as much of the liquid as possible. Cool the syrup to room temperature, transfer to a bottle or jar, and refrigerate until ready to use.

To make floats, spoon 3 tablespoons of the syrup into a tall glass and stir in ¾ cup seltzer. Add a scoop of vanilla ice cream, drizzle a little more syrup over the top, and serve.

Notes —

BAKED SPINACH CUSTARDS

Velvety smooth and creamy . . . Popeye never had it so good.

Butter, for the custard cups

1½ cups whole milk

½ cup heavy cream

3 garlic cloves, thinly sliced

1 bag (5 ounces) baby spinach, well
    washed and dried

⅓ cup packed fresh basil leaves

¾ teaspoon coarse (kosher) salt

3 large eggs

½ cup grated Parmesan cheese

Preheat the oven to 325°F.

Generously butter six 6-ounce custard cups. Line a roasting pan large enough to hold the cups in a single layer with a kitchen towel. Place the custard cups on top. Put a pan of water up to boil.

In a medium saucepan, combine the milk, cream, and garlic and bring to a simmer over low heat. Remove from the heat and stir in the spinach, basil, and salt. Cover and let stand for 2 minutes to wilt the spinach and basil.

Transfer the mixture to a blender and puree until very smooth. Add the eggs and puree until well combined.

Divide the mixture among the custard cups and scatter the Parmesan over the tops. Pour enough boiling water to come halfway up the sides of the custard cups.

Bake for 45 to 50 minutes, or until the custards are gently set. Serve either in the custard cups or run a small knife around the edges of the custards and invert onto serving plates. Serve hot or at room temperature.

Notes _____

_____

_____

ASSORTED DRESSINGS FOR YOUNG LETTUCE

MAKES VARIOUS AMOUNTS (SEE RECIPES)

We love to have a variety of salad dressings on hand, especially as the spring garden starts to give us those young, tender lettuces. It's so easy to make fresh dressings that there's really no reason to ever buy a bottle. We toss lettuce with just a bit of dressing, but how much dressing you choose to use is really a matter of taste. Start with 2 tablespoons of dressing for each 4 cups of lettuce. Another word of advice: Use a fruity olive oil without much peppery taste so the oil doesn't overpower the dressing.

CLASSIC VINAIGRETTE

2 tablespoons red wine vinegar

1/2 teaspoon coarse (kosher) salt

1 tablespoon plus 1 teaspoon Dijon
    mustard

6 tablespoons extra-virgin olive oil

SPICY TOMATO-CARROT DRESSING

1/2 cup plus 1 tablespoon extra-
    virgin olive oil

2 tablespoons minced onion

1/3 cup thinly sliced carrot

1 cup chopped tomato

1/2 cup carrot juice

3 tablespoons red wine vinegar

1/2 teaspoon chipotle chile powder

1/2 teaspoon coarse (kosher) salt

To make the classic vinaigrette: Combine all the ingredients in a half-pint (or larger) screw-top jar, cover, and shake to combine. Alternatively, whisk together the vinegar and salt. Whisk in the mustard and oil to combine. Makes 1/2 cup.

To make the spicy tomato-carrot dressing: In a small skillet, heat 1 tablespoon of the oil over medium heat. Add the onion and carrot and cook for 5 minutes, stirring frequently, until the carrot starts to soften. Add the tomato and carrot juice, cover, and simmer for 20 minutes, stirring occasionally, until the carrot is very tender. Transfer to a blender along with the remaining 1/2 cup oil, the vinegar, chipotle powder, and salt and puree until smooth. Makes 1 1/2 cups.

Notes

MANGO-CURRY DRESSING

3/4 cup diced fresh mango

2 teaspoons Madras curry powder

1/4 cup white wine vinegar

1/2 cup vegetable oil

1/2 teaspoon coarse (kosher) salt

YOGURT-HERB DRESSING

1 garlic clove, peeled

1/2 cup plain Greek yogurt
(0% to full fat, your choice)

2 tablespoons mayonnaise

2 tablespoons water

1/4 cup mixed fresh herbs, such as
flat-leaf parsley, dill, tarragon

1/2 teaspoon coarse (kosher) salt

HONEY-LIME DRESSING

1/4 cup fresh lime juice

1/2 teaspoon coarse (kosher) salt

1 tablespoon plus 1 teaspoon honey

6 tablespoons extra-virgin olive oil

To make the mango-curry dressing: In a blender, combine the mango, curry powder, vinegar, oil, and salt and puree until smooth. Makes 1 cup.

To make the yogurt-herb dressing: In a small pot of boiling water, cook the garlic for 2 minutes to remove any bitterness. Drain and transfer to a blender along with the yogurt, mayonnaise, water, herbs, and salt and puree. Makes 3/4 cup.

To make the honey-lime dressing: Combine all the ingredients in a half-pint (or larger) screw-top jar, cover, and shake to combine. Alternatively, whisk together the lime juice and salt. Whisk in the honey and oil to combine. Makes 1/2 cup.

 *Notes*

FRESH MINT SYRUP

Use this intensely flavored syrup to flavor iced tea or to spoon over cut-up fruit or a bowl of vanilla or chocolate ice cream. Or season it with a little lemon juice to make a glaze for grilled lamb. To make a terrific mint soda, add 2 to 3 tablespoons of mint syrup to 6 ounces of seltzer.

1¼ cups packed fresh mint leaves

1 cup sugar

1 cup water

In a medium saucepan of boiling water, cook the mint leaves for 10 seconds to set their color. Drain, run under cold water, and drain again. Transfer the mint to a food processor and puree.

In a small saucepan, combine the sugar and water and bring to a boil over medium heat, stirring to melt the sugar. Stir in the mint, remove from the heat, cover, and let stand for 30 minutes at room temperature.

Strain the syrup through a fine-mesh sieve set over a bowl, pushing on the solids to extract as much liquid as possible. To store, transfer to a jar or plastic container and refrigerate up to 1 month.

Notes

ARTICHOKE, FAVA BEAN, AND ASPARAGUS STEW

A perfect spring combo. Look for small baby artichokes with tightly formed heads and crisp stems.

2 pounds fava beans in the pod

2 tablespoons fresh lemon juice

1¼ pounds baby artichokes

1 tablespoon olive oil

3 cloves garlic, smashed and peeled

½ teaspoon coarse (kosher) salt

1 teaspoon finely chopped fresh
   tarragon leaves

1 pound asparagus, ends trimmed,
   cut into 1-inch lengths

2 tablespoons cold unsalted butter,
   cut up

TIDBIT: *After planting, an asparagus crown takes 4 years to fully mature. Well worth the wait!*

Remove the fava beans from their pods and discard the pods. In a large pot of boiling salted water, cook the favas for 30 seconds to blanch. Drain and run under cold water. Peel the skins off the favas (no need to do this if the favas are very small).

Add 1 tablespoon of the lemon juice to a large bowl of cold water (this is "acidulated water"). Snap off the dark outer leaves of the artichokes until you're down to paler green leaves. Trim the very bottom of the stem and, with a paring knife, remove the outer layer of the stem. Cut about ¼ inch off the tips of the artichoke leaves. Halve the artichokes lengthwise and place in the bowl of acidulated water to prevent them from discoloring.

In a large skillet, heat the oil over medium-low heat. Add the garlic and cook for 5 minutes, turning it over as it cooks, until it turns golden. Lift the artichokes out of the water and add them to the pan along with ¾ cup fresh water, the remaining 1 tablespoon lemon juice, the salt, and tarragon. Increase the heat to high, bring to a boil, then reduce to a simmer, cover, and cook for 20 to 25 minutes, turning the artichokes once or twice, until tender enough to be pierced with a knife.

Add the asparagus to the pan, cover, and cook for 3 to 5 minutes, until the asparagus are crisp-tender (timing will vary depending upon the thickness of the asparagus). Add the fava beans and cook for 1 minute to heat through. Remove from the heat and swirl in the cold butter. Serve immediately.

Notes

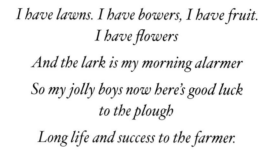

I have lawns. I have bowers, I have fruit.
I have flowers

And the lark is my morning alarmer

So my jolly boys now here's good luck
to the plough

Long life and success to the farmer.

Let the wealthy and great roll in splendor
and state,

I envy them not, I declare it

For I eat my own ham, my chicken and lamb

I shear my own fleece and wear it.

— FROM THE SONG
THE FARMER'S TOAST, 1603

SPRING RECIPES
FROM YOUR FAMILY

Summer

Summer

"The lack of power to take joy in outdoor nature is as real a misfortune as the lack of power to take joy in books."

—THEODORE ROOSEVELT

REFRIGERATOR DILLY BEANS

MAKES 2 PINTS

Y̶ou can make a refrigerator pickle out of almost anything growing in the garden, and the pickles make wonderful snacks to keep on hand throughout the summer. These crunchy beans can be stored in the refrigerator up to 2 weeks. For longer storage, they should be processed in a water bath for 10 minutes (see page 176).

1 bunch fresh dill

2 garlic cloves, peeled

1 teaspoon yellow mustard seeds

1 teaspoon dill seeds

¼ teaspoon cayenne pepper

1 pound green beans, stem ends
   trimmed

1⅓ cups cider vinegar

1⅓ cups water

2 tablespoons coarse (kosher) salt

1 tablespoon sugar

Place 2 pint-size canning jars and their lids in a pot of boiling water and heat for 1 minute. Lift out, drain, and place on the counter. Divide the fresh dill, garlic, mustard seeds, dill seeds, cayenne, and green beans between the 2 jars, packing the beans in lengthwise.

In a small saucepan, combine the vinegar, water, salt, and sugar and bring to a boil over high heat, stirring to dissolve the salt and sugar.

Pour the boiling liquid over the green beans and seal. Cool on a wire rack and refrigerate for 2 days before serving.

Notes ——————————————————————————

TOMATO JAM

S andy's mother-in-law, Margaret Stieber, who grew up on a farm in Sheboygan, Wisconsin, was a fabulous cook. Margaret was known for many great dishes, and one of the family favorites was her tomato jam. Luckily, Margaret shared it with us and now you have it, too! Try it atop a crostini spread with soft goat cheese, on a slice of toast, or on a roast beef sandwich.

3 pounds tomatoes

1 navel orange

1 lemon

1 cup sugar

$\frac{1}{2}$ teaspoon coriander seeds

$\frac{1}{2}$ teaspoon ground cinnamon

Pinch of coarse (kosher) salt

$\frac{1}{4}$ cup finely chopped crystallized ginger

With a paring knife, cut an X in the skin of each tomato. In a large pot of boiling water, blanch the tomatoes for 10 seconds to loosen the skin. Remove with a slotted spoon and run under cold water to stop the cooking.

Peel, core, halve, seed, and coarsely chop the tomatoes. Place them in a heavy-bottom medium saucepan, bring to a boil over medium heat, and cook for 10 minutes, stirring occasionally, until most of the liquid has evaporated.

With a vegetable peeler, peel the zest off the orange and lemon in wide strips. Cut the zests into thin slivers and add to the saucepan. Juice the orange and lemon and add to the saucepan. Add the sugar, coriander, cinnamon, salt, and ginger and bring to a simmer over low heat. Cook for 50 minutes, stirring frequently, until thick and glossy.

Place 2 pint-size canning jars and their lids in a pot of boiling water and heat for 1 minute. Lift out, drain, and place on the counter. Pack the hot jam into the sterilized jars and seal. Store in the refrigerator for up to 2 weeks. For longer storage, process in a water bath for 15 minutes (see page 176).

Notes

ROASTED TOMATILLO AND JALAPEÑO SALSA

Fresh tomatillos are similar in taste to green tomatoes—tangy with a hint of sweetness. Jalapeños can be tricky: Sometimes they're hot, sometimes they just taste like bell peppers. So, take a tiny bite out of the pepper and see what it's like. If you'd prefer, omit the fresh jalapeño and use a store-bought pickled jalapeño (from a jar and predictably hot) instead.

1 pound tomatillos

1 small onion, quartered

3 garlic cloves, skin on

1 jalapeño pepper

1 tablespoon olive oil

⅓ cup packed fresh flat-leaf parsley leaves

⅓ cup packed fresh cilantro leaves and tender stems

1 teaspoon ground coriander

½ teaspoon coarse (kosher) salt

TIDBIT: *The condition of the husk is often a good indicator when selecting tomatillos. If the husk is dry or shriveled, then the fruit is probably not in good condition. Select tomatillos that have an intact, tight-fitting, light brown husk. If you peel back a small part of the husk, the fruit should be firm and free of blemishes.*

Preheat the oven to 450°F.

Remove the papery husks from the tomatillos and discard. Rinse the tomatillos.

Place the tomatillos, onion, garlic, and jalapeño on a small rimmed baking sheet and drizzle with the oil. Roast for 15 minutes, shaking the pan occasionally, until the tomatillos are browned and tender.

Peel the garlic. Stem and halve the jalapeño; with a spoon or a paring knife, remove the seeds if you like your salsa mild. Cut the jalapeño into thick strips.

In a food processor, combine the parsley and cilantro and pulse until coarsely chopped. Add the tomatillos, onion, garlic, jalapeño, coriander, and salt and pulse until coarsely chopped. To store, transfer to a container, cover, and refrigerate up to 3 days.

Notes _____

_____

_____

ROASTED NEW POTATOES BAKED IN A SALT CRUST

SERVES 4

The "french fry" was allegedly served in the United States for the first time by Thomas Jefferson at a presidential dinner, but if we had been allowed to choose the potato for that meal, we would have offered this Beekman 1802 dish instead. The rosemary, coriander, and mustard seeds impart a little flavor without taking over, and a salt crust keeps the potatoes underneath moist and very tender. Serve as is or, if you like, add a little butter.

2 tablespoons olive oil

10 whole fresh rosemary sprigs

1 tablespoon grated lemon zest

1 tablespoon plus 1 teaspoon
    coriander seeds

2 teaspoons yellow mustard seeds

1¼ pounds small new potatoes,
    scrubbed

2½ cups coarse (kosher) salt

2 large egg whites

1 tablespoon fresh lemon juice

Preheat the oven to 400°F.

Coat a 9-inch pie plate with the oil. Scatter the rosemary, lemon zest, coriander, and mustard seeds in the bottom of the pan. Top with the potatoes.

In a medium bowl, stir together the salt, egg whites, and lemon juice and scrape the mixture over the potatoes, patting to cover the potatoes (no need to come to the edges of the pan). Bake for 1 hour 15 minutes, or until the potatoes are tender.

To serve, crack the salt coating and lift the potatoes out.

 *Notes*

PIERINO'S BELL PEPPERS

Sandy first tasted these tender, sweet, salty, basil-scented peppers at Ristorante Gambero Rosso in Cesenatico, Italy. Pierino Giovene is the chef who created the dish. Choose thick-walled peppers (such as Holland bell peppers) for this dish. Sicilian Castelvetrano olives are meaty and sweet, with a hint of brine.

2 large red or yellow bell peppers

1 plum tomato, cored and finely chopped

¼ cup pitted Castelvetrano or Spanish Manzanilla olives, coarsely chopped

¼ cup fresh basil leaves, finely chopped

1 garlic clove, minced

2 anchovy fillets, mashed

2 tablespoons capers

2 tablespoons olive oil

TIDBIT: *A bell pepper's sugar content increases as the fruit ripens on the plant, so the green varieties, which are picked earlier, are the least sweet and sometimes even have an almost bitter taste to them. The red, orange, and yellow peppers are the sweetest.*

Preheat the oven to 350°F. Line a rimmed baking sheet with parchment paper.

Cut ½ inch off the tops of the peppers, finely chop the tops, and transfer to a medium bowl. Cut the peppers into 4 flat panels, then cut each in half crosswise. Arrange, skin-side down, on the baking sheet.

Add the tomato, olives, basil, garlic, anchovies, and capers to the bowl with the chopped pepper tops. Spoon the mixture onto the peppers and drizzle the tops with the oil.

Cover the baking sheet with foil and bake for 25 minutes. Uncover and bake for 10 minutes longer, or until the peppers are tender.

Notes

SPICY TOMATO SAUCE

B eekman 1802 is famous for its Mortgage Lifter tomato sauces that give back 25 percent of the profits to help other small farms pay off their mortgages. This version of the sauce has a surprising twist: mango, which adds a hint of exotic, natural sweetness. Use the sauce as a dipping sauce for fries, or mix with a little mayo and use it as a sandwich spread (it's great with chicken).

2 garlic cloves, peeled

1½ pounds tomatoes

1 small mango, cut into small
  chunks (¾ cup)

1 long green hot pepper or 3 to 4
  jalapeño peppers, ribs and seeds
  removed and coarsely chopped
  (¼ cup)

⅓ cup white wine vinegar

3 tablespoons light brown sugar

1 teaspoon coarse (kosher) salt

In a medium saucepan of boiling water, blanch the garlic for 1 minute. Lift out with a slotted spoon and transfer to a blender. Leave the water boiling.

With a paring knife, cut an X into the skin of each tomato. Add the tomatoes to the boiling water and blanch for 10 seconds to loosen the skin. Drain and rinse under cold water, then peel, core, and coarsely chop.

Add the tomatoes to the blender along with the mango, hot pepper, vinegar, brown sugar, and salt and puree until smooth.

Transfer the mixture to a medium saucepan and bring to a boil over medium heat. Reduce to a simmer, cover, and cook, stirring occasionally, for 10 minutes, or until thick and reduced to 2 cups. Store in the fridge, where it'll keep up to 2 weeks.

Notes

TOMATO TART

The tomato was not widely accepted as a food until the 19th century; now 93 percent of American gardening households grow tomatoes. This tart recipe will help you make up for any lost time. Tomatoes and creamy ricotta: good in pasta, great on pizza, but perfect in a tart.

All-purpose flour, for rolling the pastry

1 sheet (7 to 8 ounces) frozen all-butter puff pastry, thawed but still cold

2 tablespoons olive oil

1 cup whole-milk ricotta, drained

4 ounces soft goat cheese, crumbled

2 large eggs

1/3 cup chopped fresh basil

3/4 teaspoon coarse (kosher) salt

1/4 teaspoon freshly ground black pepper

3/4 pound tomatoes, cored, halved, and cut into 1/2-inch-thick slices

Preheat the oven to 425°F. Line a baking sheet with parchment paper.

On a lightly floured work surface, roll the pastry out to a 10 × 15-inch rectangle and transfer it to the baking sheet.

With a paring knife, score a border 1 inch in from the edge all around the rectangle, cutting into, but not through, the dough. With a fork, prick the dough inside the border all over (this is so the border will rise higher than the center that's been pricked). Brush the center with 1 tablespoon of the oil.

In a large bowl, stir together the ricotta, goat cheese, eggs, basil, 1/2 teaspoon of the salt, and the pepper. Spread the mixture over the center of the puff pastry sheet. Top with the tomatoes, overlapping slightly. Sprinkle the tomatoes with the remaining 1/4 teaspoon salt and the remaining 1 tablespoon oil.

Bake for 30 minutes, or until the pastry is golden brown and the filling is set.

Notes _____

SUMMER SQUASH LASAGNA ROLLS

SERVES 6

In our first bestselling cookbook, *The Beekman 1802 Heirloom Cookbook,* one of the most popular recipes for autumn was the Butternut Squash–Filled Lasagna Rolls, so we couldn't help but come up with an equally delicious version for the summer squash that is always so plentiful. Although there are a few brands of lasagna noodles that are short and wide, be sure to use the more typical long lasagna noodles here, for ease of rolling. The yellow summer squash for the filling is roasted here, but if it's warm weather and you've got the grill going, use it instead: Lightly brush the grates with oil and grill the squash until tender.

1 pound yellow summer squash, cut lengthwise into $\frac{1}{2}$-inch-thick slabs

3 tablespoons olive oil

1 teaspoon coarse (kosher) salt

6 lasagna noodles

1 cup whole-milk ricotta cheese

$\frac{1}{2}$ cup grated Parmesan cheese

$\frac{1}{2}$ cup packed basil leaves, finely chopped

$\frac{1}{4}$ cup sun-dried tomatoes, finely chopped

1 large egg

1 pound tomatoes, cored and diced

Preheat the oven to 400°F.

Place the squash slabs on a rimmed baking sheet. Brush with 2 tablespoons of the oil and sprinkle with $\frac{1}{2}$ teaspoon of the salt. Roast for 20 minutes, turning the squash over midway, until very tender. Remove the squash but leave the oven on. Reduce the oven temperature to 350°F.

Meanwhile, in a large pot of boiling water, cook the lasagna noodles to al dente, according to package directions. Drain and transfer to a bowl of cold water to keep the noodles from sticking together.

In a medium bowl, blend together the ricotta, Parmesan, basil, sun-dried tomatoes, and egg. Lay the noodles out on a work surface and spread the ricotta mixture over, dividing it evenly. Top with the squash. Starting at one short end, roll up the noodles.

Scatter half of the diced fresh tomatoes in the bottom of a 9 × 9-inch baking dish. Place the lasagna rolls on top, seam-side down. Top with the remaining fresh tomatoes, sprinkle with the remaining $\frac{1}{2}$ teaspoon salt, and drizzle the remaining 1 tablespoon oil on top.

Cover and bake for 30 to 35 minutes, or until the tomatoes are bubbling and the lasagna rolls are piping hot. Serve immediately.

Notes

BLOODY MARY SOUP

Cucumber vodka gives the soup a very fresh taste, but if you can't find it, any vodka will do. That said, this can also be a Virgin Bloody Mary Soup; just leave the vodka out and swap in ⅓ cup of water. Refrigerator Dilly Beans (page 75) make a fun and tasty garnish. For the smoothest soup, use a blender rather than a food processor.

2 pounds beefsteak tomatoes, cored and coarsely chopped

2 scallions, thinly sliced

1 celery stalk, thinly sliced

3 tablespoons finely chopped poblano or red bell pepper

2 tablespoons Worcestershire sauce

1½ tablespoons white horseradish, homemade (page 52) or store-bought

3 tablespoons fresh lemon juice

1 tablespoon cayenne pepper sauce, such as Frank's RedHot

½ teaspoon coarse (kosher) salt

⅓ cup cucumber vodka (see Tidbit) or plain vodka

TIDBIT: *To make your own cucumber vodka, peel and cut one English cucumber and allow to steep in a bottle of vodka for 3 days.*

In a blender, combine the tomatoes, scallions, celery, poblano, Worcestershire, horseradish, lemon juice, hot sauce, and salt and pulse to combine. Add the vodka and puree until very smooth. Transfer to a container and chill until very cold. Serve in glasses.

Notes

BRUSCHETTA WITH 3 TOPPINGS

Most people think of bruschetta as having a tomato-based topping, but just like pesto, a bruschetta topping can be made of virtually anything and is a great use for ripe or even overly ripe summer vegetables. Traditionally bruschetta are made by grilling slices of bread over coals and then rubbing them with garlic. We've chosen a simpler method in which the bruschetta are baked in the oven. Three topping suggestions follow, each making enough to cover 8 pieces of bread. Other topping ideas we like are soft goat cheese topped with some Tomato Jam (page 76); cream cheese with Blaak Onion Jam Chutney (page 213); or a good oil-packed Spanish or Italian tuna, a squeeze of lemon, and a vine-ripened summer tomato.

BRUSCHETTA

1 baguette (10 ounces), cut into
   $\frac{1}{2}$-inch-thick slices (about 24)

$\frac{1}{3}$ cup olive oil

2 garlic cloves, peeled and halved

1 teaspoon coarse (kosher) salt

CREAMY KALE TOPPING

2 tablespoons olive oil

1 garlic clove, thinly sliced

2 anchovy fillets, very finely
   chopped

6 ounces kale, stems and ribs
   discarded

$\frac{1}{4}$ teaspoon coarse (kosher) salt

$\frac{1}{2}$ cup water

2 tablespoons mayonnaise

2 tablespoons grated Parmesan
   cheese

2 teaspoons fresh lemon juice

To make the bruschetta: Preheat the oven to 350°F.

Place the slices of baguette on a large rimmed baking sheet and brush both sides with the oil. Bake for 10 to 12 minutes, turning the slices over midway, until golden brown and crisp. Remove from the oven, rub the cut side of the garlic cloves over one side of each slice. Sprinkle with the salt.

To make the kale topping: In a large skillet, heat the oil over medium heat. Add the garlic and anchovies and cook for 2 minutes, stirring frequently, until the anchovies have melted. Add the kale, salt, and water and cook for 5 to 7 minutes, stirring frequently, until the kale is tender and the water has evaporated. When cool enough to handle, finely chop.

Meanwhile, in a medium bowl, combine the mayonnaise, Parmesan, and lemon juice.

Add the kale mixture to the mayonnaise mixture and stir to combine. Divide the mixture among 8 toasts.

continued

Notes

SMOKED SALMON TOPPING

3 ounces cream cheese

$1\frac{1}{4}$ teaspoons drained white horseradish, homemade (page 52) or store-bought

1 teaspoon grated lemon zest

$1\frac{1}{2}$ ounces thinly sliced smoked salmon, cut into 8 pieces

$\frac{1}{4}$ cup finely diced tomato

$\frac{1}{4}$ cup minced red onion

2 tablespoons snipped fresh dill

1 teaspoon small (nonpareil) capers, rinsed

1 teaspoon olive oil

$\frac{1}{4}$ teaspoon fresh lemon juice

$\frac{1}{8}$ teaspoon coarse (kosher) salt

ROASTED PEPPER TOPPING

$\frac{1}{2}$ cup roasted red peppers, homemade (see Tidbit, page 118) or store-bought, finely chopped

2 tablespoons chopped pitted Gaeta or kalamata olives

2 tablespoons chopped fresh mint leaves

1 tablespoon olive oil

$\frac{1}{2}$ teaspoon coarse (kosher) salt

To make the smoked salmon topping: In a small bowl, combine the cream cheese, horseradish, and lemon zest. Spread 2 teaspoons of the mixture on each of 8 toasts and top each with a piece of smoked salmon. Put a tiny dollop of the remaining cream cheese mixture on top of the salmon.

In a small bowl, combine the tomato, onion, dill, capers, oil, lemon juice, and salt. Divide the mixture among the bruschetta.

To make the roasted pepper topping: In a small bowl, combine the peppers, olives, mint, oil, and salt. Divide the mixture among 8 toasts.

Notes

SUMMER VEGETABLE FLANS

When entertaining summer guests at the farm, we often like to serve a "conversation starter" at the start of the meal. This silky custard studded with vegetables really gets people talking.

1 tablespoon olive oil, plus more for the custard cups

1 shallot, finely chopped

2 garlic cloves, finely chopped

1 cup finely diced zucchini

1/2 teaspoon coarse (kosher) salt

1 cup fresh corn kernels

3 ounces feta cheese, crumbled

3 large eggs

3/4 cup whole milk

3/4 cup heavy cream

Preheat the oven to 350°F. Brush six 6-ounce custard cups or ramekins with oil. Put a pot of water up to boil.

In a large skillet, heat the 1 tablespoon oil over medium heat. Add the shallot and garlic and cook for 2 minutes, stirring, until tender. Stir in the zucchini and salt and cook for 7 minutes, stirring occasionally, until the zucchini is tender. Stir in the corn and cook 1 minute longer.

Place the custard cups in a baking pan large enough to hold them in a single layer. Line the pan with a kitchen towel. Divide the vegetable mixture among the custard cups and scatter the feta over the top.

In a medium bowl, whisk together the eggs, milk, and cream. Divide the mixture among the custard cups. Pour the boiling water into the baking pan to come halfway up the sides of the cups. Bake the flans for 25 minutes, until the custard is just set. Remove from the water bath, let cool 5 minutes, then run a metal spatula around the edge of the cups and invert the flans onto serving plates. (Or, if you prefer, you can leave the flans in the cups and serve them that way.)

Notes

GREEN BEANS WITH FRIZZLED SCALLIONS AND GINGER

Beekman 1802 Farm is a place where city often meets country. Having had plates of green beans much like this in many a Chinese restaurant during our days in Manhattan, we decided to try them at home and were more than pleasantly surprised at how well they turned out. For best and sweetest flavor, look for crisp, not-too-thick green beans. If you like, switch it up by using some wax beans and some green beans.

1 pound green beans, stem ends
   trimmed

2 tablespoons extra-virgin olive oil

¾ teaspoon coarse (kosher) salt

Vegetable oil

4 scallions, tender green and white
   parts, thinly sliced lengthwise
   (½ cup)

3 inches fresh ginger, thinly sliced
   and then cut into matchsticks
   (¼ cup)

In a large pot of boiling salted water, cook the green beans for 4 minutes until crisp-tender (timing will vary depending on the thickness of the beans). Drain well and toss with the olive oil and ½ teaspoon of the salt. Transfer to a serving platter.

Meanwhile, pour ½ inch of vegetable oil into a small saucepan and heat over medium heat to 360°F on a deep-frying thermometer. (Alternatively, if you don't have a thermometer, drop a little flour into the oil; if it sizzles, the oil is ready.) Add the scallions and ginger and cook for 2 minutes, or until the scallions are beginning to brown but are still mostly green. Scoop them out with a slotted spoon or spider and transfer to a paper towel-lined plate to drain. Set the oil aside.

To serve, spoon 2 tablespoons of the scallion-ginger oil over the green beans, top with the frizzled scallions and ginger, and sprinkle with the remaining ¼ teaspoon salt.

Notes

CORN CAKE STACKS WITH
AGED CHEDDAR AND ARUGULA

When corn is in season, use it for these mouthwatering stacks. For easy cleanup, line the kitchen sink with newspaper and strip the husk and silk off the cobs over the sink. When finished, gather the paper around the husk and silk and throw it all away or compost it. To strip the kernels off the cob, stand it upright in a large shallow bowl and, with a chef's knife, cut down to release the kernels.

2 cups corn kernels, fresh (from about 2 ears) or frozen and thawed

¼ cup finely diced red bell pepper

2 tablespoons cornmeal

1 teaspoon sugar

¾ teaspoon coarse (kosher) salt

¼ teaspoon baking powder

2 large eggs, separated

4 tablespoons olive oil

1½ cups shredded aged Cheddar cheese (6 ounces)

2 cups baby arugula

TIDBIT: *An ear of corn averages 800 kernels in 16 rows. Each silk protruding from the top is attached to an individual kernel.*

Preheat the oven to 350°F.

In a large bowl, stir together the corn, bell pepper, cornmeal, sugar, salt, baking powder, and egg yolks.

In a separate bowl, with an electric mixer, beat the egg whites to stiff peaks. Fold the egg whites into the corn mixture.

In a large skillet, heat 2 tablespoons of the oil over medium heat. Working in batches, drop half the batter by scant ¼-cup mounds into the oil, flattening them slightly with a spatula, and cook for 2 minutes per side, or until golden brown. Transfer to a baking sheet and repeat with the remaining batter and 2 tablespoons oil.

Divide the Cheddar among the corn cakes and bake for 1 minute, just until the cheese has melted. Remove from the oven, top each with some of the arugula, and then stack 3 together making a total of 4 stacks. Serve immediately.

Notes

THE MAIN BARN AT
BEEKMAN 1802 FARM

CORN CHESS PIE

From Landreth's Heirloom Seed Catalog: "Sweet corn, the kind with which most of us are familiar, differs from all other types of corn because the kernels lack the ability to convert their sugars to starch, giving the corn a sweeter taste." So. Corn for dessert? Why not? The combo of sugar, eggs, and cream along with pureed corn makes for a wonderful, custardy pie.

CRUST

3/4 cup all-purpose flour (spooned into cup and leveled off), plus more for rolling

1/2 cup cornmeal

1/4 cup sugar

1/4 teaspoon baking powder

1/4 teaspoon salt

4 tablespoons cold unsalted butter, cut up

1 large egg

1 teaspoon distilled white vinegar

FILLING

1 3/4 cups sugar

3 tablespoons cornmeal

1/4 teaspoon salt

8 tablespoons (1 stick) unsalted butter, melted and cooled

1 1/4 cups corn kernels, fresh (from 1 to 2 ears) or thawed frozen

4 large eggs

1/4 cup heavy cream

1 tablespoon distilled white vinegar

To make the crust: In a food processor, combine the flour, cornmeal, sugar, baking powder, and salt. Add the butter and pulse until the mixture resembles coarse crumbs. Add the egg and vinegar and pulse until combined. Transfer to a sheet of wax paper and flatten to a 1/2-inch-thick disk. Refrigerate for at least 1 hour or up to overnight. Freeze for longer storage.

Preheat the oven to 400°F.

On a lightly floured work surface, roll out the dough to an 11-inch round. Roll the dough around the rolling pin and then fit it into a 9-inch pie plate without stretching it, pressing the dough into the bottom and against the sides of the pan. With a pair of scissors or a paring knife, trim the dough to leave a 1-inch overhang all around. Fold the overhang in over the rim to make a double layer of dough and, with your fingers, crimp the dough all around.

Line the pie shell with foil or parchment paper, leaving an overhang, and fill with pie weights or dried beans to weight the crust down. Bake for 10 minutes, then remove the foil and weights and bake for 10 minutes longer, until the crust is almost set. Remove the pie shell but leave the oven on. Reduce the oven temperature to 350°F.

Meanwhile, to make the filling: In a food processor, combine the sugar, cornmeal, and salt. Add the butter, corn, eggs, cream, and vinegar and puree.

Pour the filling into the partially baked pie shell and bake for 55 minutes, or until the custard is just set. Cool to room temperature before serving, or refrigerate and serve chilled.

Notes _____

GRILLED TINY CORN

Who doesn't love the summery flavors found in fresh salsa and warm tortillas? Throw in a margarita and you have an instant party, even if there are only two people celebrating. This twist on a South-of-the-Border street-food classic will make the evening a fiesta to remember (and talked about the next day). Grilled corn, with a variety of toppings—mayo and cotija cheese (a mild, firm Mexican cheese) being musts—is known as *elote* in Mexico where it is sold on many a street corner. Here we use baby corn, grill it, and then serve the toppings as a dip.

1 can (15 ounces) baby corn, rinsed and drained

1 tablespoon olive oil

$\frac{1}{2}$ teaspoon coarse (kosher) salt

$\frac{1}{4}$ cup mayonnaise

$\frac{1}{4}$ cup grated cotija or Parmesan cheese

1 teaspoon fresh lime juice

$\frac{1}{2}$ teaspoon chili powder

$\frac{1}{4}$ teaspoon ground coriander

Preheat a grill (with a grill topper) or grill pan to medium heat.

In a medium bowl, toss the corn with the oil and $\frac{1}{4}$ teaspoon of the salt. Grill, turning the corn as it colors, 2 to 3 minutes per side, until grill marks appear and the corn is very hot.

In a serving bowl, stir together the mayonnaise, cotija or Parmesan, lime juice, chili powder, coriander, and the remaining $\frac{1}{4}$ teaspoon salt.

Serve the corn with fun toothpicks and the dipping sauce.

Notes _____

VEGETABLE-PACKED MAC AND CHEESE WITH POPCORN TOPPING

SERVES 6

Summer brings out the kid in all of us, and what dish is more pleasing to kids than mac and cheese? This gave us the perfect opportunity to act like kids ourselves and get playful. We thought, Hey, why not top a mac and cheese with popcorn instead of bread crumbs? And for an extra cheesy twist, why not make it store-bought cheese popcorn?

2 cups cavatappi pasta

4 tablespoons (½ stick) unsalted butter

1 cup finely chopped onion

1 cup shredded carrots

1 medium yellow squash, halved lengthwise and thinly sliced

2 plum tomatoes, cored and coarsely chopped

3 cups shredded extra-sharp Cheddar cheese

½ cup sour cream

½ cup whole milk

2 large eggs

1 teaspoon coarse (kosher) salt

½ teaspoon freshly ground black pepper

2 cups cheese popcorn, lightly crushed

Preheat the oven to 400°F.

In a large pot of boiling salted water, cook the pasta 2 minutes shy of the time in the package directions. Drain and transfer to a large bowl. Add 3 tablespoons of the butter and toss to coat.

Meanwhile, in a medium saucepan, heat the remaining 1 tablespoon butter over medium heat. Add the onion and cook for 7 minutes, stirring occasionally, until tender and starting to color. Add the carrots and squash and cook for 5 minutes, or until the carrots are tender. Add the tomatoes and cook for 1 minute longer.

Transfer the sautéed vegetables to the bowl with the pasta. Add 2 cups of the Cheddar, the sour cream, milk, eggs, salt, and pepper and stir until well combined. Transfer the mixture to a 9 × 9-inch baking dish and scatter the remaining 1 cup Cheddar on top. Top with the popcorn.

Bake for 25 minutes, or until the pasta is piping hot and the top is lightly crusted. Serve immediately.

Notes

GRILLED STEAK AND LIMA BEAN SALAD

Lima beans (along with other pod beans) are a labor of love. For each pound in the pod, you get about 1 cup shelled beans. We've gone ahead and used frozen limas here to spare you the chore, but when fresh are around and you've got the time, give them a try.

2 tablespoons plus 2 teaspoons olive oil, plus more for the grill

1 teaspoon garam masala

$\frac{1}{2}$ teaspoon coarse (kosher) salt

$\frac{1}{4}$ teaspoon freshly ground black pepper

$1\frac{1}{4}$ pounds hanger, skirt, or flank steak

1 package (10 ounces) frozen baby lima beans

3 tablespoons red wine vinegar

$2\frac{1}{2}$ teaspoons Dijon mustard

$\frac{1}{2}$ cup finely chopped red onion

1 Kirby cucumber, peeled and cut into $\frac{1}{2}$-inch cubes

1 small head frisée (see Tidbit), torn into bite-size pieces (4 cups), or baby arugula

TIDBIT: *Frisée is a member of the chicory family and can range from mild to very bitter. We love the contrast here between the sharp Dijon, the vinegar, and the sweet-starchy limas, but feel free to swap in your favorite green.*

Preheat a grill or grill pan to medium. Lightly oil the grates or grill pan.

In a large bowl, combine the garam masala, salt, and pepper. Rub 1 teaspoon of the mixture into both sides of the steak. Rub the steak with 2 teaspoons of the oil.

Place the steak on the grill and grill for 3 minutes per side for rare (or, if you prefer, longer for more well done). Let rest for 10 minutes before thinly slicing against the grain.

Meanwhile, in a small pot of boiling water, cook the limas according to package directions. Drain well, rinse under cold water, and drain again.

Add the vinegar, mustard, and remaining 2 tablespoons oil to the bowl with the reserved garam masala mixture and whisk together to combine. Add the limas, onion, cucumber, steak, and frisée, and toss to combine.

Notes ———————————

GOLDEN GAZPACHO WITH MINTED CREAM

This chilled soup is a summer treasure chest.

1 pound yellow tomatoes, cored and cut into large chunks

1 yellow bell pepper, cut into large chunks

1 yellow squash (4 ounces), cut into large chunks

2 shallots, peeled and halved

1 cup carrot juice

2 tablespoons sherry wine vinegar

¾ teaspoon coarse (kosher) salt

½ cup fresh mint leaves

½ cup sour cream

TIDBIT: *All peppers start out green, and as they mature they acquire their vibrant colors and varying flavors. This change in color is caused by the breakdown in chlorophyll (the green coloring) as the fruit matures.*

In a blender, combine the tomatoes, bell pepper, squash, shallots, carrot juice, vinegar, and salt and puree until smooth. Transfer to a container and refrigerate until chilled.

In a small saucepan of boiling water, cook the mint leaves for 10 seconds to set the color. Drain and rinse under cold water. Squeeze dry and finely chop. Transfer to a small bowl with the sour cream and stir to combine.

Serve the soup in chilled bowls with a dollop of minted sour cream in each.

Notes —————

Roasting the corn kernels and adding some chipotle chile powder to the soup gives it a slightly smoky taste. The corncobs have some sweet corn flavor, and their broth gives the soup an extra corn boost that will take your breath away.

3 ears corn, husked

1 poblano pepper, cut into ¼-inch dice

1 small red bell pepper, cut into ¼-inch dice

2 tablespoons olive oil

3 cups water

2 tablespoons unsalted butter

½ cup finely chopped red onion

2 garlic cloves, thinly sliced

¼ teaspoon chipotle chile powder

¾ teaspoon coarse (kosher) salt

½ cup heavy cream

TIDBIT: *The Native American word* maiz *means "sacred mother" or "giver of life." Some ancient tribes believed that corn is afraid to be cooked, so a woman must warm it first with her breath.*

Preheat the oven to 375°F.

Using a chef's knife, scrape the corn kernels off the cobs onto a rimmed baking sheet; reserve the cobs. Add the poblano and bell pepper to the baking sheet, drizzle with the oil, and roast for 25 minutes, tossing the vegetables once or twice, until the corn is lightly browned.

Meanwhile, cut the cobs into thirds crosswise and place in a medium saucepan with the water. Bring to a boil over high heat, reduce to a simmer, cover, and cook for 20 minutes, or until the liquid is flavorful. Strain the corn broth into a bowl.

In a large saucepan, heat the butter over medium heat. Add the onion and garlic and cook for 7 minutes, stirring occasionally, until the onion is tender. Add the roasted corn and pepper mixture, the corn broth, chipotle powder, and salt and simmer for 5 minutes for the flavors to blend. Add the cream and gently heat. Serve hot.

Notes _____

SWEET CUCUMBER-BUTTERMILK SORBET IN A CARROT COOKIE CUP

Carrots have a higher sugar content than any other vegetable except the sugar beet, so we added just a little bit of carrot juice to the cookies for the natural sweetness. The refreshing sorbet (no one will guess it's made from cucumbers) is delicious on its own, but if you serve it with the carrot cookies, you get two vegetables in one dessert!

SORBET

3/4 cup sugar

3/4 pound mini (aka Persian) cucumbers, thinly sliced

3 tablespoons honey

1 tablespoon fresh lime juice

2 cups buttermilk

CARROT LACE COOKIES

3/4 cup pecans

1/2 cup sugar

1 1/2 tablespoons all-purpose flour

1/8 teaspoon salt

4 tablespoons (1/2 stick) unsalted butter

3 tablespoons carrot juice

To make the sorbet: In a medium saucepan, bring the sugar and cucumbers to a simmer over medium-low heat. Cover and cook for 5 minutes, or until very tender. Transfer to a food processor and puree. Strain through a fine-mesh sieve into a bowl.

Stir the honey, lime juice, and buttermilk into the cucumber puree. Refrigerate until chilled, transfer to an ice cream machine, and process according to the manufacturer's directions. Serve right away or freeze.

To make the cookies: Preheat the oven to 375°F. Line a baking sheet with parchment. Set 3 custard cups, upside down, on the kitchen counter.

In a food processor, combine the pecans, sugar, flour, and salt and pulse until the pecans are finely ground.

In a medium saucepan, cook the butter and carrot juice over medium heat until the butter has melted. Stir in the nut mixture and cook for 2 minutes, stirring until lightly thickened and bubbling.

Drop 3 cookies onto the baking sheet using 1 tablespoonful of batter and spacing them several inches apart. With dampened fingers, flatten the cookies to a 2-inch round. Bake for 10 minutes, or until set around the edges and lightly browned. Let cool on the baking sheet for 1 minute, then with a thin-bladed metal spatula, transfer each still-warm and flexible cookie to a custard cup and press to shape around the cup. Remove when cooled. Repeat with the remaining batter, making 3 cookies each time.

To serve, remove the sorbet from the freezer 20 minutes before serving to soften. Scoop the sorbet into cookie cups and serve immediately.

 *Notes*

SUMMER PICNIC PASTA SALAD

Fresh herbs, sun-drenched tomatoes, and corn make for a simple pasta salad that just screams summer. If you'd like to jazz the salad up, add some cheese (goat, feta, or mozzarella) and toasted nuts (pine nuts or almonds). You can make this ahead and refrigerate it, but if you do, two things: Bring it back to room temperature before serving and taste for salt, adding more if necessary.

½ pound farfalle pasta

¼ cup extra-virgin olive oil

3 garlic cloves, peeled and lightly smashed

¾ pound plum tomatoes, cored and diced

1 cup corn kernels, fresh (about 1 ear) or thawed frozen

⅓ cup fresh basil leaves, finely chopped

¼ cup fresh mint leaves, finely chopped

1 teaspoon coarse (kosher) salt

In a large pot of boiling salted water, cook the pasta according to package directions. Drain.

Meanwhile, in a small saucepan, heat the oil over low heat. Add the garlic and cook for 7 minutes, stirring occasionally, until golden brown and very tender. Reserving the oil, remove the garlic and finely chop.

Pour the garlic oil into a large bowl and add the chopped garlic, drained pasta, tomatoes, corn, basil, mint, and salt and toss to combine. Serve at room temperature.

Notes

LIMA BEAN SOUP WITH CORN GARNISH

L ima beans seem to be one of those love 'em or hate 'em vegetables. As a southerner, Brent grew up eating succotash. And we *both* love limas, fresh or frozen. We decided to use frozen here to make this succotash-inspired summer soup super easy.

2 tablespoons olive oil

1 small onion, finely chopped

1 baking potato, peeled and diced

2 packages (10 ounces each) frozen lima beans (no need to thaw)

3 cups chicken broth

¼ cup snipped fresh dill, plus sprigs for garnish

2 teaspoons chopped fresh tarragon leaves

¾ teaspoon coarse (kosher) salt

¼ teaspoon freshly ground black pepper

1 ear corn, husked

¼ cup roasted red pepper, finely diced

TIDBIT: *To make your own roasted peppers: Cut 1 red bell pepper vertically into flat panels. Place them, skin-side up, on a broiler pan and broil for 10 minutes, or until the skin is blackened. Transfer the peppers to a plate, skin-side down. When cool enough to handle, peel. This should give you ¹/₂ cup roasted pepper.*

In a medium saucepan, heat the oil over medium heat. Add the onion and potato and cook for 7 to 10 minutes, stirring frequently, until the onion is tender. Add the lima beans, broth, dill, tarragon, salt, and pepper and bring to a boil. Reduce to a simmer, cover, and cook for 10 minutes, or until the lima beans are very tender.

Meanwhile, with a chef's knife, scrape the corn kernels off the cob. In a small pot of boiling water, cook the corn for 30 seconds. Drain.

Once the limas are tender, scoop out 2 cups of the mixture and puree in a food processor. Return the puree to the soup and stir to combine.

Serve the soup with the corn, roasted pepper, and dill sprigs on top.

Notes

GRILLED BEET SALAD WITH RICOTTA, WATERCRESS, AND ALMONDS

S mall beets (just a wee bit smaller than a golf ball) are sweet like candy and are a nice contrast to the spicy watercress and milky ricotta. And save those beet greens—you can sauté them the way you would spinach or use them in place of the kale in the creamy kale topping (page 92) for bruschetta.

12 small beets (1 pound total), well scrubbed

3 tablespoons extra-virgin olive oil, plus more for the grill

1½ tablespoons red wine vinegar

½ teaspoon coarse (kosher) salt

¼ teaspoon freshly ground black pepper

1 bunch watercress, tough stems discarded (about 4 cups)

¼ cup snipped fresh dill

¼ cup sliced almonds

1 cup whole-milk ricotta cheese

In a vegetable steamer, cook the beets for 10 minutes, or until they start to give when squeezed between your fingers. Remove from the steamer and when cool enough to handle, peel the beets by holding a paper towel in your hand and rubbing the skin off. Halve the beets.

Preheat a grill or a grill pan to medium. Oil the grill grates (or the pan). If the grates on your grill are widely spaced, place a grill topper on it and oil the grill topper.

In a large bowl, whisk together the oil and vinegar for the dressing. Add the beets and toss to coat. Lift the beets from the dressing and set the remaining dressing aside. Place the beets on the grill, the topper, or the grill pan and grill for 7 to 10 minutes, turning them as they get grill marks, until fork-tender.

Add the salt and pepper to the reserved dressing along with the watercress, beets, dill, and almonds and toss to combine. Divide the mixture among 4 serving plates and top each with ¼ cup ricotta. Serve immediately.

Notes _____

THE "MILKMAIDS" AT
BEEKMAN 1802 FARM

PARMESAN-PACKED EGGPLANT MEATBALLS

Brent's not a huge fan of eggplant, but he'll eat it if it's accessorized. Here it's been dolled up with Parmesan and herbs and shaped into tender "meatballs." Like many of the recipes created on the farm, this one was perfected over time. After several tries, we decided the best way to cook these was to shape them and pop them in the oven where they firm up. They're good on their own, served with a dipping sauce (try a combo of yogurt and herbs), or topped with your favorite tomato sauce and served over pasta.

1¹/₂ pounds firm small eggplants, peeled and cut into 1-inch chunks

2 garlic cloves, peeled

2 tablespoons olive oil

1 teaspoon coarse (kosher) salt

¹/₂ cup fresh flat-leaf parsley leaves

¹/₃ cup fresh basil leaves

1 cup panko bread crumbs

²/₃ cup grated Parmesan cheese

2 large eggs

TIDBIT: *If an eggplant is fresh, when you press your finger against it, the fingerprint will disappear quickly.*

Preheat the oven to 350°F.

In a small baking pan, toss the eggplant and garlic with the oil. Sprinkle with ¹/₂ teaspoon of the salt, cover with foil, and bake for 30 minutes, or until tender but not mushy. (Leave the oven on and increase the temperature to 375°F.) When the eggplant is cool enough to handle, squeeze to get rid of excess liquid.

In a food processor, pulse the parsley and basil until coarsely chopped. Add the eggplant, garlic, panko, Parmesan, eggs, and the remaining ¹/₂ teaspoon salt and pulse to combine (it will still be a little chunky).

Line a rimmed baking sheet with parchment paper. With a small ice cream scoop (¹/₄ cup), scoop the mixture into 12 meatballs. With dampened hands, round the meatballs out and place on the baking sheet. Bake for 25 to 30 minutes, or until firm.

Notes _____

_____

_____

GOLDEN SQUASH, PEPPER, AND TOMATO GRATIN

Golden squash, bright yellow in color, is a sweet member of the summer squash family (think yellow squash, zucchini, and a host of others), so feel free to swap in any of them, especially in the height of summer when they're taking over the garden. While this is great right out of the oven, it also makes a terrific picnic dish.

3 tablespoons olive oil

1 medium red onion, finely chopped

2 garlic cloves, thinly sliced

2 golden squash, yellow squash, or zucchini, cut into 1/4-inch-thick rounds

1 red bell pepper, cut into 1-inch squares

3/4 teaspoon coarse (kosher) salt

1/4 cup fresh basil leaves, finely chopped

1/2 cup plus 2 tablespoons grated Parmesan cheese

1 pound tomatoes, cored and thickly sliced

1/2 cup panko bread crumbs

Preheat the oven to 375°F.

In a large skillet, heat 2 tablespoons of the oil over medium heat. Add the onion and garlic and cook for 7 minutes, stirring occasionally, until the onion is tender.

Add the squash and bell pepper, sprinkle with 1/2 teaspoon of the salt, and cook for 7 to 10 minutes, stirring occasionally, until the squash is tender. Stir in the basil and 2 tablespoons of the Parmesan.

Spoon the mixture into a 9 × 9-inch baking dish. Top with the tomato slices and sprinkle with the remaining 1/4 teaspoon salt. Scatter the panko and the remaining 1/2 cup Parmesan over the top and drizzle with the remaining 1 tablespoon oil. Bake for 20 minutes, or until the topping is crisp and the vegetables are piping hot. Serve hot or at room temperature.

Notes —

God said, "I need somebody strong enough to clear trees and heave bails, yet gentle enough to tame lambs and wean pigs and tend the pink-combed pullets, who will stop his mower for an hour to splint the broken leg of a meadow lark. It has to be somebody who plows deep and straight and does not cut corners. Somebody to seed, weed, feed, breed and rake and disc and plow and plant and tie the fleece and strain the milk and replenish the self-feeder and finish a hard week's work with a 5-mile drive to church.

"Somebody who'd bale a family together with the soft strong bonds of sharing, who would laugh and then sigh, and then reply, with smiling eyes, when his son says he wants to spend his life 'doing what dad does.'"

So God made a farmer.

—PAUL HARVEY, 1978

SUMMER RECIPES
FROM YOUR FAMILY

Fall

SIX OF OUR LEADING VEGETABLE SPECIALTIES:

25¢

RADISH-ICICLE

CUCUMBER-DAVIS PERFECT

LETTUCE-HANSON

BEET MAU BLO TUR

PEPPER CHINESE GIANT

ONE COLLECTION

Fall

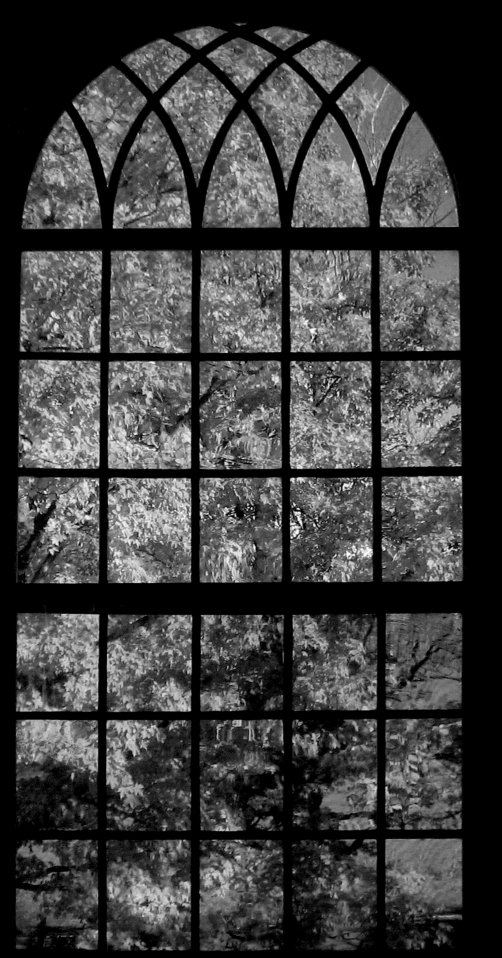

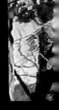
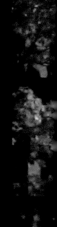

"Tickle [the earth] with a hoe and she laughs with a harvest."

—DOUGLAS JERROLD

ROASTED CARROT AND CAULIFLOWER SALAD

For a slightly fancier presentation, "roll-cut" the carrots: Place a cooked carrot on a work surface and make one $^1\!/_2$-inch cut on the diagonal. Roll the carrot over and make another cut, then continue cutting and rolling the carrot until it's all cut.

$^1\!/_4$ cup olive oil

$^3\!/_4$ pound carrots (about 3 carrots)

$^3\!/_4$ pound cauliflower, cut into large florets

3 garlic cloves, skin on

1 tablespoon fresh lemon juice

$^1\!/_2$ teaspoon coarse (kosher) salt

$^1\!/_3$ cup coarsely chopped fresh flat-leaf parsley

TIDBIT: *The carrot greens should be removed prior to storing a carrot in the refrigerator. The greens wilt quickly, and as they wilt, they siphon away moisture from the vegetable.*

Preheat the oven to 400°F.

Pour the oil into a roasting pan. Add the carrots, cauliflower, and garlic and toss to coat. Roast for 25 minutes, turning the carrots and cauliflower over as they brown, until the cauliflower is tender enough to be pierced with a knife. Remove the cauliflower and transfer to a large bowl. If the carrots are still a little hard, give them another 5 to 10 minutes of cooking time.

When the carrots are cool enough to handle, slice into $^1\!/_2$-inch-thick rounds and transfer to the bowl. Peel the garlic, mash it, and add it to the bowl along with the lemon juice, salt, and parsley. Serve at room temperature.

Notes

SMOKY BROCCOLI RABE

Broccoli rabe, because it's somewhat bitter, is a challenge for some folks. We love it any which way, but cooked with smoky paprika and sun-dried tomatoes is one of our favorites. Great as a side dish, it's also perfect tossed with pasta and a handful of grated Parmesan cheese.

2 tablespoons olive oil

3 garlic cloves, very thinly sliced

1½ teaspoons sweet smoked paprika

1 bunch broccoli rabe (1 pound), ends trimmed, cut into ½-inch-wide slices (10 cups)

½ teaspoon coarse (kosher) salt

¼ cup plump sun-dried tomatoes, coarsely chopped

¼ cup water

TIDBIT: *Cool weather brings out the best in this vegetable, mellowing its harsh edge slightly. Depending on where you shop, you may also see it labeled as broccoli raab, rapini, or cima di rapa.*

In a large skillet, warm the oil over very low heat. Add the garlic and cook very gently for 10 minutes, or until meltingly tender.

Add the smoked paprika and cook for 1 minute. Add the broccoli rabe, adding it in handfuls as it wilts, and sprinkle with the salt.

Add the sun-dried tomatoes and water and increase the heat to medium. Cover and cook for 7 minutes, or until the broccoli rabe is tender but not mushy. Serve warm.

Notes _____

_____

_____

ROASTED MASHED POTATOES WITH GOAT CHEESE

Sandy's mom always added cream cheese to her mashed potatoes. We've taken liberties, and because we raise goats and make goat cheese at Beekman 1802 Farm, we used it in place of the cream cheese. We've left just a little bit of skin on the potatoes for some texture, but feel free to take it off. Potatoes can vary in how dry they are, so once they've been mashed, add more milk (or, of course, cheese!) if you want them creamier.

1¾ pounds russet (baking) potatoes, well scrubbed, peeled in stripes, and quartered (lengthwise and crosswise)

3 garlic cloves, peeled

3 scallions, thinly sliced

2 tablespoons olive oil

1 teaspoon coarse (kosher) salt

¾ cup plus 2 tablespoons whole milk

1 log (3½ to 4 ounces) soft goat cheese

Preheat the oven to 400°F.

In a 9 × 13-inch baking pan, toss the potatoes with the garlic, scallions, oil, and ½ teaspoon of the salt. Cover with foil and bake for 30 minutes, or until the potatoes are tender.

In a large saucepan, combine the milk, goat cheese, and the remaining ½ teaspoon salt and bring to a simmer over low heat. Add the potatoes, garlic, and scallions and coarsely mash.

Notes

COLLARD GREENS AND APPLE WITH HOT DRESSING

When Brent was growing up, collard greens were served at least once a week, either at Grandma's house or on the school lunch menu. They were usually boiled with a ham hock and served with vinegar. While Brent swears this is the purest way to appreciate them, over the years we've come up with some variations that also suit him just fine.

2½ tablespoons olive oil

2 shallots, minced

2 garlic cloves, thinly sliced

2 bunches (1¼ pounds total) collard greens, stems removed, leaves cut into 1-inch-wide ribbons (see Tidbit) and well washed

2 teaspoons sugar

½ teaspoon coarse (kosher) salt

1 sweet/tart apple, peeled and thinly sliced

2 tablespoons cider vinegar

1 tablespoon Dijon mustard

TIDBIT: *The easiest and fastest way to cut collards into ribbons is by stacking them, rolling them up like a cigar, and then cutting them crosswise. And don't worry if a little bit of water is still clinging to the leaves after washing; it'll cook off.*

In a large skillet, heat 1½ tablespoons of the oil over medium-low heat. Add the shallots and garlic and cook for 5 minutes, stirring frequently, until the shallots are tender. Add the collard greens, ½ teaspoon of the sugar, and the salt and cook for 15 minutes. Add the apple and continue cooking for 15 minutes, stirring occasionally, until the collards are very tender. Transfer to a large serving bowl.

Add the remaining 1 tablespoon oil to the skillet and heat over medium heat. Add the remaining 1½ teaspoons sugar, the vinegar, and mustard and bring to a boil. Pour the hot dressing over the collards, toss to coat, and serve.

Notes

CARAMELIZED ONION AND POTATO HAND PIES

On rainy autumn days, we often make up "storage" foods that we can whip out when unexpected company comes calling. These savory hand pies are perfect for snacking or entertaining. They can be frozen and baked straight from the freezer. To bake from frozen, increase the baking time by 5 to 10 minutes.

DOUGH

1½ cups all-purpose flour (spooned into cup and leveled off), plus more for rolling

2 teaspoons sugar

¼ teaspoon salt

8 tablespoons (1 stick) cold unsalted butter, cut into bits

½ cup Greek yogurt (2% or higher)

FILLING

1 tablespoon olive oil

1 tablespoon unsalted butter

2 cups chopped onions

1 russet (baking) potato (about 10 ounces), peeled and thinly sliced

2 tablespoons plain whole-milk Greek yogurt

¾ teaspoon coarse (kosher) salt

1 large egg

1 tablespoon water

To make the dough: In a food processor, pulse the flour, sugar, and salt. Add the butter and pulse until the mixture resembles coarse crumbs. Add the yogurt and pulse just until combined (the dough should hold together when pinched between your fingers). Divide the dough into quarters, wrap each in plastic wrap, and flatten to rectangles. Refrigerate for at least 1 hour or up to a day. For longer storage, freeze up to 3 months.

To make the filling: In a large skillet, heat the oil and butter over medium-low heat. Add the onions and cook for 25 minutes, stirring frequently, until golden brown and very tender.

Meanwhile, in a small saucepan of boiling salted water, cook the potato for 10 minutes, or until tender. Drain well, transfer to a bowl, and mash with a potato masher.

Stir the onions, yogurt, and salt into the mashed potatoes.

Preheat the oven to 325°F. Line a baking sheet with parchment paper.

Working with one piece of dough at a time, on a lightly floured work surface, roll the dough to a 5 × 12-inch rectangle. Halve the dough crosswise to make two 5 × 6-inch rectangles. With a short end facing you, place ¼ cup of the potato filling on the bottom half, leaving a ½-inch border. Brush the border with water, fold the top over, and pinch to seal. Repeat with the remaining dough and filling. Place on the baking sheet and make several slashes in the tops of the hand pies.

In a small bowl, beat together the egg and water. Brush the tops of the hand pies with the egg wash. Bake for 35 minutes, or until the tops are golden brown and crisp. Transfer to a wire rack to cool for 5 minutes before serving.

 Notes ————————————————

CHOW-CHOW

This time-honored condiment goes with just about anything. We love it alongside fried chicken, as a side for slow-cooked beans, as a topping for burgers, and even on a fish taco. And for a slightly different take, add 1 cup coarsely chopped fresh pineapple to the mixture as it's cooking. We've processed the chow-chow by heating the jars in a water bath for longer storage. If you know you'll be eating the relish in a few weeks, simply store it in the fridge and you can skip the processing step.

3 cups chopped green cabbage

3 cups chopped green tomatoes

2 cups chopped onion

1 medium red bell pepper, coarsely chopped

1 medium green bell pepper, coarsely chopped

2 cups distilled white vinegar

1 cup sugar

2 tablespoons coarse (kosher) salt

8 pickled jalapeño slices

2 bay leaves

2 cinnamon sticks, split lengthwise

1 teaspoon coriander seeds

1 teaspoon yellow mustard seeds

8 allspice berries

In a large saucepan or Dutch oven, bring the cabbage, tomatoes, onion, red and green bell peppers, vinegar, sugar, salt, jalapeño, bay leaves, cinnamon, coriander seeds, mustard seeds, allspice berries, and 4 cups of water to a boil over high heat. Reduce to a simmer, partially cover, and cook for 30 minutes, or until the vegetables are very tender.

Meanwhile, in a large pot of boiling water, sterilize four 1-pint canning jars and their lids.

Spoon the vegetables into the hot sterilized jars, leaving ½ inch of headroom, and seal with the lids. Process in a water bath for 10 minutes (see page 176). Remove the jars from the water bath and place on a wire rack to cool. The chow-chow will keep for several months in a cool location.

Notes _____

_____

_____

SWISS CHARD PIE WITH PINE NUTS AND RAISINS

SERVES 8 TO 10

Josh learned a lot of his cooking skills and love for food from his uncle who lived in a small village outside of Arles. In this part of the south of France, this pie is both sweet and savory. While traditionally it's made with an olive oil crust, we decided to use phyllo instead to make it easier. When working with phyllo, keep the sheets that you aren't working with covered in either plastic wrap or a dampened paper towel, or they will dry up quickly.

FILLING

2 pounds Swiss chard, stems
    discarded, well washed

2 tablespoons unsalted butter

1 Bartlett pear, peeled, cored, and
    coarsely chopped

2 large eggs

1/2 cup heavy cream

1/2 cup plus 2 tablespoons
    granulated sugar

1/2 cup golden raisins

1/3 cup pine nuts, toasted

1/3 cup grated Parmesan cheese

1 1/2 teaspoons grated orange zest

PIE

8 tablespoons (1 stick) unsalted
    butter, melted

10 sheets (9 x 14-inch) phyllo dough

2 tablespoons confectioners' sugar

To make the filling: Roll the Swiss chard leaves up like a cigar and thinly slice lengthwise and crosswise. In a large skillet, heat the butter over medium heat. Add the pear and chard and cook for 20 minutes, stirring occasionally, until the pear and chard are tender. Transfer to a large bowl and cool to room temperature. Stir in the eggs, cream, granulated sugar, raisins, pine nuts, Parmesan, and orange zest.

To make the pie: Preheat the oven to 350°F.

Brush a 9-inch round cake pan with some of the melted butter. Brush 1 sheet of phyllo with butter and place in the pan, butter-side up. Brush another sheet and stack it on top of the other, also butter-side up. Repeat with 3 more sheets of phyllo, stacking them in the pan, butter-side up, so that the entire bottom of the pan is covered. Spoon the filling into the pan.

Repeat the brushing and stacking of the phyllo, using another 5 sheets and this time placing them in the pan butter-side down, leaving an equal overhang on 2 sides. Tuck the overhang into the pan to enclose the filling and brush the top sheet of phyllo with the remaining butter.

Bake for 25 to 30 minutes, or until the top is golden brown and crisp. Cool to room temperature in the pan on a wire rack. To serve, invert the cooled pie onto a serving plate and dust with the confectioners' sugar.

Notes —

BAKED PARMESAN STEAK FRIES
WITH TOMATO DIPPING SAUCE

SERVES 4

Yes. You *can* dress up french fries for grown-ups. This version makes a nice addition to autumn tailgating.

2 russet (baking) potatoes (8 to 10 ounces each), peeled and each cut lengthwise into 8 wedges

¼ cup olive oil

⅔ cup grated Parmesan cheese

⅓ cup ketchup

2 anchovy fillets, finely chopped and mashed

1 teaspoon red wine vinegar

Coarse (kosher) salt

TIDBIT: *A 30-minute soak in ice water helps the potatoes get nice and crisp without deep-frying.*

Place the potatoes in a bowl of ice water and let stand for 30 minutes (see Tidbit). Drain well and pat dry with paper towels.

Preheat the oven to 450°F.

Place the potatoes on a large rimmed baking sheet. Drizzle with oil and toss to coat. Sprinkle the Parmesan over the potatoes and bake for 25 minutes. With a thin-bladed metal spatula, turn the potatoes over and bake for 10 minutes longer, or until the potatoes are crisp on the outside and tender within.

Meanwhile, in a small bowl, stir together the ketchup, anchovies, and vinegar.

Transfer the fries to a plate lined with paper towels and sprinkle with salt to taste. Serve hot, with the ketchup dipping sauce on the side.

Notes ———

LEEK AND WALNUT TART

Gruyère, an assertive, sweet, nutty Swiss cheese is our choice for this savory tart. The combination of flavors here may be just what you need to cure any end-of-summer blues.

DOUGH

1¼ cups all-purpose flour (spooned into cup and leveled off)

1 tablespoon sugar

¼ teaspoon salt

8 tablespoons (1 stick) cold unsalted butter, cut into bits

3 to 4 tablespoons ice water

FILLING

2 tablespoons unsalted butter

3 medium leeks, halved lengthwise, cut into ½-inch-wide slices, well washed, and dried

¾ teaspoon coarse (kosher) salt

¼ teaspoon freshly ground black pepper

½ cup heavy cream

1 large egg

⅛ teaspoon cayenne pepper

1 cup shredded Gruyère cheese (4 ounces)

¼ cup walnuts, coarsely chopped

To make the dough: In a large bowl, whisk together the flour, sugar, and salt. With a pastry blender or 2 knives used scissor-fashion, cut in the butter until large pea-size bits are formed. Add just enough ice water so the mixture holds together when pinched between the fingers. Shape into a disk, wrap in wax paper or plastic wrap, and refrigerate for at least 1 hour or up to 2 days. For longer storage, freeze up to 3 months.

Preheat the oven to 400°F.

On a lightly floured work surface, roll the dough to a 12-inch round. Fit it into a 9-inch round tart pan with a removable bottom, pressing it into the bottom and up the sides of the pan and making a high edge that comes about ½ inch over the top. Roll a rolling pin across the top of the tart to make a neat edge; discard the excess dough.

With a fork, prick the bottom of the dough all over. Line the tart shell with foil, leaving an overhang, and fill with pie weights to weight the crust down. Bake for 15 minutes, or until starting to crisp, then remove the foil and weights and bake 10 minutes longer, or until golden brown and crisp. Remove from the oven and set aside.

To make the filling: In a large skillet, heat the butter over medium-low heat. Add the leeks, sprinkle with the salt and black pepper and cook for 15 to 20 minutes, stirring occasionally, until very soft. Transfer to a large bowl and cool to room temperature.

Add the cream, egg, and cayenne to the bowl and mix well. Scatter half the Gruyère in the bottom of the tart shell. Scrape the leek mixture into the tart shell. Scatter the walnuts and remaining Gruyère over the top and bake for 25 to 30 minutes, or until the custard is set. Transfer to a wire rack to cool for 10 minutes before removing the tart from the pan. Serve hot or at room temperature.

 Notes _____

PENNE WITH MUSHROOMS, WINTER SQUASH, AND BROWN BUTTER

Juniper berries are the surprise ingredient in this earthy dish. They give gin its particular flavor and, when used along with woodsy mushrooms and piney rosemary, make this dish robust. When you think of warming fall flavors, this has them all.

2 tablespoons olive oil

1 medium red onion, finely chopped

3 garlic cloves, thinly sliced

1/2 pound fresh shiitake mushrooms, stems discarded and caps quartered

1/2 pound white mushrooms, trimmed and thickly sliced

1 1/4 pounds kabocha squash, peeled and cut into 1-inch chunks (about 1/2 squash)

3/4 teaspoon coarse (kosher) salt

3/4 teaspoon crumbled dried rosemary

12 juniper berries, crushed with the flat side of a knife

1 cup chicken broth

1/2 pound penne or other short tubular pasta

4 tablespoons (1/2 stick) unsalted butter

1/2 cup grated Parmesan cheese

In a large skillet, heat the oil over medium heat. Add the onion and garlic and cook for 7 to 10 minutes, stirring occasionally, until the onion is tender. Add the shiitake and white mushrooms and cook for 5 minutes, stirring frequently, until the mushrooms are tender.

Add the squash, salt, rosemary, and juniper berries and stir to combine. Add the broth, cover, and cook for 10 to 12 minutes, stirring occasionally, until the squash is tender.

Meanwhile, in a large pot of boiling water, cook the pasta according to package directions. Drain and transfer to a large bowl.

When the squash mixture is done, add it to the pasta.

In a small skillet, melt the butter over medium heat. Cook for 1 to 2 minutes, or until the butter foams, then subsides and turns brown in spots. Pour the butter over the pasta mixture, add the Parmesan, and toss to combine.

Notes ——————————————————

ROASTED CAULIFLOWER "STEAKS"
WITH ORANGE-OLIVE SAUCE

Josh and Brent both grew up as "meat and potato" guys in "meat and potato" families. Now they only eat proteins that they raise in the pastures of Beekman 1802. The garden is a much more convenient and plentiful pantry, and the true inspiration for this recipe.

1 head cauliflower (about 2¼ pounds)

¼ cup olive oil

2 garlic cloves, skin on

2 inches fresh ginger, skin on, thinly sliced

½ teaspoon coarse (kosher) salt

⅓ cup orange marmalade

¼ cup black or green olives, pitted and coarsely chopped

1 tablespoon plus 1 teaspoon Dijon mustard

1 tablespoon plus 2 teaspoons red wine vinegar

½ teaspoon ground coriander

TIDBIT: *You will have florets that fall off when you make the "steaks." Just toss them with a little olive oil and roast them in a small baking pan when you bake the steaks. Save them for a snack or toss them into a salad.*

Preheat the oven to 400°F.

Cut off the bottom stem end of the cauliflower so that it will sit flat on a work surface. Slice the cauliflower vertically into 4 thick slabs (see Tidbit). Transfer to a rimmed baking sheet.

In a small skillet, heat the oil over low heat. Add the garlic and ginger and cook for 5 to 7 minutes, or until the garlic is golden brown.

Strain the oil through a fine-mesh sieve into a bowl, pushing on the solids to extract as much oil as possible. Drizzle the oil over the cauliflower and sprinkle with the salt.

Bake for 30 to 35 minutes, turning the cauliflower over once, until tender.

Meanwhile, in a medium bowl, stir together the marmalade, olives, mustard, vinegar, and coriander.

Serve the cauliflower with the orange-olive sauce spooned over.

Notes ———————————————————

BUTTERED KOHLRABI

In German, the word *kohlrabi* translates roughly as "cabbage turnip." While the name doesn't sound very appetizing, and the vegetable itself looks a little like something from outer space, kohlrabi is crisp and delicious. There are many varieties out there, but our favorite is the Kossak—it's big (it can weigh 5 pounds), sweet, and not at all woody. The kohlrabi's unique name and odd appearance have kept this vegetable off of American tables for far too long. Let's change that!

1½ pounds kohlrabi

3 tablespoons unsalted butter

¾ teaspoon coarse (kosher) salt

¾ cup water

With a paring knife, peel the kohlrabi. Cut it in half, then cut it into ½-inch-thick slices. Cut the slices into ½-inch-wide french fry shapes.

Place the kohlrabi in a large skillet along with the butter, salt, and water. Bring to a boil over high heat, reduce to low, cover, and simmer for 10 minutes. Uncover and cook for 5 minutes, or until the water has evaporated and the kohlrabi is tender and coated with butter. Serve hot.

 Notes _____

FRIED POLENTA WITH SAUTÉED SPINACH

SERVES 4

The polenta can be made a day or two ahead and refrigerated until ready to sauté. If you prefer, you can swap in a store-bought log of already prepared polenta (flavored or plain), cut it crosswise into 8 slices, and sauté it in olive oil until crisp before topping it with the sautéed spinach.

4 tablespoons olive oil, plus more
  for the pan

4 cups water

1 cup plus 2 tablespoons cornmeal

2 teaspoons coarse (kosher) salt

²/₃ cup grated Parmesan cheese

2 tablespoons unsalted butter

¹/₂ teaspoon grated orange zest

1 garlic clove, thinly sliced

1¹/₄ pounds baby spinach

1 teaspoon sugar

2 tablespoons orange juice

Brush an 8 × 8-inch baking pan with oil.

In a medium bowl, stir together 2 cups of the water and the corn-meal. In a large heavy saucepan, bring the remaining 2 cups water and 1 teaspoon of the salt to a boil over high heat. Whisk in the dampened cornmeal, reduce the heat to medium-low, and cook for 20 minutes, whisking frequently, until the cornmeal is tender and thick. Whisk in the Parmesan, butter, orange zest, and ¹/₂ teaspoon of the salt until combined. Pour the polenta into the prepared bak-ing pan, spreading it to an even layer. Cool to room temperature, then refrigerate for 1¹/₂ hours until firm.

Run a small knife around the sides of the baking pan and invert the polenta onto a work surface. Cut the polenta into four 4-inch squares.

In a large nonstick skillet, heat 1¹/₂ tablespoons of the oil over medium heat. Add half the polenta and cook for 2 to 3 minutes per side, or until golden brown and crisp. Repeat with another 1¹/₂ tablespoons oil and the remaining polenta. Transfer to 4 plates.

In another large skillet, heat the remaining 1 tablespoon oil over medium heat. Add the garlic and cook for 2 minutes, or until soft but not browned. Add the spinach, sugar, and the remaining ¹/₂ teaspoon salt and cook for 1 minute, stirring, until wilted. Sprinkle the orange juice over the spinach, tossing to combine.

Serve the polenta topped with the spinach.

Notes

BASIC PICKLED GARLIC, SHALLOTS, OR GROUND CHERRIES

One year we judged the pickle competition at our county fair, and one of the Grand Prize entries that truly stood out was pickled peaches—sweet, tangy, and totally unexpected. We love when people get a little creative, so we thought we'd do a little Pickling 101. There are two basic ways of putting up pickles: One way is to make them in small batches and keep them in the fridge; the other involves canning in a water bath, which allows you to keep whatever you've just pickled at room temperature for at least a year. Either of these methods works for garlic, shallots, pearl onions, carrots, cauliflower, and a host of other vegetables and fruits. See what you come up with.

PICKLED GARLIC

2 bulbs garlic (6 ounces total), separated into cloves and peeled

3 sprigs fresh thyme

½ cup distilled white vinegar

½ cup water

2½ teaspoons coarse (kosher) salt

PICKLED SHALLOTS

½ pound shallots, peeled and halved if large

2 bay leaves

1 large sprig fresh sage

¾ cup red wine vinegar

¾ cup water

1 tablespoon sugar

2½ teaspoons coarse (kosher) salt

To make the pickled garlic: In a large pot of boiling water, sterilize a half-pint canning jar and its lid. Pack the garlic and thyme into the sterilized jar.

In a small saucepan, combine the vinegar, water, and salt and bring to a boil, stirring until the salt has dissolved. Pour the boiling mixture over the garlic, leaving ½ inch of headroom. Seal with the lid. Process in a water bath (see page 176) or cool to room temperature and refrigerate up to 1 month.

To make the pickled shallots: In a large pot of boiling water, sterilize a 1-pint canning jar and its lid. Pack the shallots, bay leaves, and sage into the sterilized jar.

In a small saucepan, combine the vinegar, water, sugar, and salt and bring to a boil, stirring until the salt has dissolved. Pour the boiling mixture over the shallots, leaving ½ inch of headroom. Seal with the lid. Process in a water bath (see page 176) or cool to room temperature and refrigerate up to 1 month.

continued on page 176

 Notes _____

PICKLED GROUND CHERRIES

½ pound ground cherries, husks
   removed

2 bay leaves

1 large sprig fresh sage

¾ cup red wine vinegar

¾ cup water

1 tablespoon sugar

2½ teaspoons coarse (kosher) salt

TIDBIT: *Ground cherries, also known as cape gooseberries or husk tomatoes, taste a little like a cross between a tomato and a berry. They come wrapped in a husk, similar to that on a tomatillo. Depending on where you live, they're in season anytime from the end of July into the fall.*

To make the pickled ground cherries: In a large pot of boiling water, sterilize a 1-pint canning jar and its lid. Pack the ground cherries, bay leaves, and sage into the sterilized jar.

In a small saucepan, combine the vinegar, water, sugar, and salt and bring to a boil, stirring until the salt has dissolved. Pour the boiling mixture over the ground cherries, leaving ½ inch of headroom. Seal with the lid. Process in a water bath (see below) or cool to room temperature and refrigerate up to 1 month.

****

TO PROCESS IN A WATER BATH: *Place a wire rack in the bottom of a large, deep pan—wide enough to hold the jars without touching one another or the sides of the pan, and deep enough for water to cover the jars by 2 inches. Place the jars in the pan, add very hot water to cover by 2 inches, bring to a boil, and boil for 10 minutes (or as your recipe directs). Remove the jars from the water bath and cool on a wire rack. Store in a cool, dry place, out of the light, for up to a year.*

Notes _____

_____

_____

KALE WITH BACON, SAGE, AND POTATOES

Kale can be a prolific member of the autumn garden, and we are always looking for ways to play up both its sweetness and its sturdiness. In this recipe, the leaf really pulls it all together.

1 russet (baking) potato
   (10 ounces), peeled and cut into
   ½-inch chunks

1 tablespoon olive oil

4 slices smoky bacon (about
   4 ounces)

3 garlic cloves, peeled and smashed

1 bunch kale (1 pound), stems and
   ribs discarded, leaves thinly
   sliced

¾ teaspoon coarse (kosher) salt

½ teaspoon finely chopped fresh
   sage

2 tablespoons water

In a large pot of boiling salted water, parcook the potatoes for 5 minutes (they'll cook more later). Drain.

In a large skillet, heat the oil over medium heat. Add the bacon and cook for 7 to 10 minutes, turning it over as it cooks, until crisp. Remove with tongs. Leave the bacon fat in the pan. When cool enough to handle, break the bacon into small pieces.

Add the garlic to the bacon fat in the pan and cook for 2 minutes, or until it starts to color. Add the potatoes, kale, salt, sage, and water and cook for 15 to 20 minutes, stirring occasionally, until the kale is very tender and the potatoes are cooked through. Add the bacon and serve.

 Notes

BEEKMAN 1802 SWEET POTATO AND MARSHMALLOW CASSEROLE

Who hasn't seen a version of this classic sitting on an autumn dinner table? We like to use a mix of both regular sweet potatoes (the orange-fleshed ones) and the white Japanese variety that tend to be a little drier than the others. Feel free to use whichever ones you like. Sandy remembers that her Aunt Syl always brought the sweet potato casserole to Thanksgiving. This one, somewhat different than the traditional, gets a smoky kick from ancho chile powder, a little tang from lime juice, and a tropical flavor from both the coconut and the coconut milk.

3 pounds sweet potatoes

1/2 cup coconut milk

3 tablespoons maple syrup, preferably dark

1 teaspoon ancho chile powder

1 tablespoon fresh lime juice

1 1/2 teaspoons coarse (kosher) salt

1/3 cup sweetened flaked coconut

1 cup mini marshmallows

TIDBIT: *What is the difference be-tween a sweet potato and a yam? Afri-can slaves in the South called the sweet potato nyami because it reminded them of the starchy, edible tuber of that name that grew in their homeland. The Senegalese word nyami was eventually shortened to the word yam. Yam also refers to sweet potatoes grown in Louisi-ana. You can use sweet potatoes and yams interchangeably in most recipes.*

Preheat the oven to 425°F. Line a baking sheet with foil or parch-ment paper (for easier cleanup).

Prick the sweet potatoes in several places, place on the baking sheet, and bake for 1 hour, or until tender. Leave the oven on but reduce the temperature to 350°F.

When cool enough to handle, peel the potatoes and transfer them to a large bowl. Add the coconut milk, maple syrup, chile powder, lime juice, and salt and mash (if you prefer a super smooth texture, use a handheld or a stand mixer to mash the potatoes).

Spoon the mixture into a 9 × 9-inch baking dish and bake for 30 minutes, or until piping hot.

Meanwhile, in a small dry skillet, toast the coconut over low heat for 2 to 3 minutes, shaking the pan frequently, until lightly golden.

Scatter the marshmallows over the top of the sweet potatoes and sprinkle with the toasted coconut. Bake for 5 minutes, or until the marshmallows have melted.

Notes

CHOPPED SALAD

Chopped salads can be made from any variety of vegetables and lettuces as long as there's a mix of soft and crunchy textures. One of the best chopped salads in New York City is from Fred's at Barney's New York department store. It is said to have been developed because the ladies who often lunched there found it easier to eat than salads with larger pieces of lettuce.

1 cup buttermilk

$\frac{1}{4}$ cup mayonnaise

2 tablespoons sour cream

2 tablespoons chopped parsley

2 tablespoons fresh lemon juice

1 teaspoon coarse (kosher) salt

1 medium red bell pepper, cut into $\frac{1}{2}$-inch squares

1 medium yellow bell pepper, cut into $\frac{1}{2}$-inch squares

1 plum tomato, cored, halved, seeded, and cut into $\frac{1}{2}$-inch cubes

1 cucumber, halved lengthwise, seeded and cut into $\frac{1}{2}$-inch cubes

$\frac{1}{4}$ cup finely diced red onion

1 can (15.5 ounces) chickpeas, drained and rinsed

1 Hass avocado, cut into $\frac{1}{2}$-inch chunks

2 cups chopped romaine lettuce

2 cups chopped buttercrunch lettuce

In a large bowl, whisk together the buttermilk, mayo, sour cream, parsley, lemon juice, and salt.

Add the bell peppers, tomato, cucumber, onion, chickpeas, avocado, and lettuce and toss to combine.

Notes

BEET CHOCOLATE CAKE WITH CANDIED BEET TOPPING

Sugar beets account for about one-third of the world's supply of sugar, and their relative, the red beet, is no slouch in the sugar department either. So it's not as odd to use them in a chocolate cake as you might think. While we've made this with fresh beets, you can make it with canned beets—just be careful that they're not pickled! You'll need two 15-ounce cans to get the 1½ cups puree. Candied beets are a nice, fun touch, but the cake is still delicious with just the chocolate glaze.

CAKE

1¾ pounds red beets

8 ounces (2 sticks) unsalted butter, melted, plus softened butter for the pan

¼ cup sifted unsweetened cocoa powder, plus more for the pan

1¼ cups all-purpose flour (spooned into cup and leveled off)

1½ teaspoons baking soda

¼ teaspoon salt

3 large eggs

1 cup granulated sugar

½ cup packed light brown sugar

1 teaspoon pure vanilla extract

3 ounces semisweet chocolate, melted

To make the cake: Preheat the oven to 350°F.

Halve the beets lengthwise, place on a sheet of foil, and wrap the foil around the beets. Place the beets on a baking sheet and bake for 35 to 40 minutes, or until tender. When cool enough to handle, using a paper towel, rub the skin off. Transfer to a food processor and puree until smooth. You'll need 1½ cups of puree for the cake; if you've got leftovers, serve them as a side dish with a little butter or olive oil and salt.

Butter the bottom and sides of a 9 × 13-inch baking pan and line the bottom with wax paper. Butter the paper and dust the pan with cocoa powder.

In a bowl, stir together the flour, ¼ cup cocoa powder, the baking soda, and salt.

In a separate bowl, with an electric mixer, beat the eggs, both sugars, the melted butter, and vanilla until well combined. Beat in the pureed beets and chocolate. Fold in the flour mixture until just combined.

Pour the batter into the prepared pan and smooth the top. Bake for 35 to 40 minutes, or until the cake just starts to pull away from the sides of the pan and a wooden pick inserted in the center comes out with just a few moist crumbs attached.

continued

Notes _____

_____

_____

CANDIED BEET TOPPING

$2/3$ cup sugar

$1/3$ cup water

1 tablespoon fresh lemon juice

2 candy stripe beets (about 6 ounces total), peeled and very thinly sliced crosswise

CHOCOLATE GLAZE

8 ounces semisweet chocolate, coarsely chopped

4 tablespoons unsalted butter, cut into bits

1 tablespoon honey

TIDBIT: *Candy stripe beets (also called chioggia) are actually striped white and red. They taste just like regular beets, but make a really pretty presentation.*

Cool in the pan on a wire rack, then run a metal spatula around the sides and invert onto a serving platter or the wire rack.

To make the candied beets: In a small saucepan, combine the sugar, water, and lemon juice and cook over low heat, stirring until the sugar has dissolved. Add the beets and cook for 25 minutes, stirring occasionally, until the beets are translucent. Lift the beets out of the syrup and transfer to a wire rack to cool completely.

To make the chocolate glaze: In a medium bowl set over, not in, a pan of simmering water, melt the chocolate. Remove from the heat and stir in the butter and honey. Cool, stirring occasionally, until the glaze is of a spreading consistency. Spread on the cooled cake and top with the candied beets.

Notes ——————————————

STEWED GREEN BEANS WITH POTATO AND TOMATO

SERVES 4

Brent has never been able to replicate the taste of his grandmother's stewed beans and potatoes, which she made in the cooler months from beans she had "put up" earlier in the summer. After tasting this dish in a Greek diner, he proclaimed it a close second. The green beans will not stay bright green, but they become meltingly tender in this traditional Greek dish.

2 tablespoons olive oil

1 ounce fatback, cut into small pieces

1 cup finely chopped onion

3 garlic cloves, thinly sliced

$1\frac{1}{2}$ cups coarsely chopped tomatoes

1 pound green beans, stem ends trimmed

$\frac{1}{2}$ pound small boiling potatoes, peeled and cut into 1-inch chunks

1 tablespoon tomato paste

$\frac{1}{4}$ cup chopped fresh flat-leaf parsley

$\frac{1}{4}$ cup chopped fresh mint

$\frac{1}{4}$ cup snipped fresh dill

$\frac{3}{4}$ teaspoon coarse (kosher) salt

$\frac{1}{4}$ teaspoon freshly ground black pepper

$\frac{1}{2}$ teaspoon grated lemon zest

$1\frac{1}{2}$ cups water

2 tablespoons fresh lemon juice

In a large saucepan or Dutch oven, heat the oil over medium heat. Add the fatback and cook for 5 minutes, stirring occasionally, until it starts to crisp up. Add the onion and garlic and cook for 7 minutes, stirring occasionally, until the onion is tender. Add the tomatoes and cook for 5 minutes, or until they start to get saucy.

Stir in the green beans, potatoes, tomato paste, parsley, mint, dill, salt, pepper, lemon zest, and water and bring to a boil. Reduce to a simmer, cover, and cook for 45 minutes, or until the beans are very tender. Stir in the lemon juice and serve hot.

Notes

CANDIED FENNEL AND FRIED LEMONS

The sweet licorice-like fennel and the tart, slightly bitter lemon make for a nice contrast in flavors and textures. A great side dish to serve with seafood.

½ cup plus 1 tablespoon sugar

½ cup water

2 fennel bulbs, stalks discarded, bulb cut lengthwise through the core into ½-inch-thick slices

1½ teaspoons fennel seeds

⅓ cup all-purpose flour

1 large egg beaten with 1 tablespoon water

½ cup panko bread crumbs

1 lemon, thinly sliced into rounds, seeds discarded

3 tablespoons vegetable oil

½ teaspoon coarse (kosher) salt

In a large skillet, combine ½ cup of the sugar and the water and bring to a boil over high heat, stirring until the sugar has dissolved. Add the fennel and fennel seeds, reduce to a simmer, and cook for 10 minutes, or until tender. Transfer to a wire rack set over a baking sheet or a sheet of wax paper to catch any drips. Sprinkle the remaining 1 tablespoon sugar over the slices.

Set up 3 shallow bowls. Place the flour in one, the egg mixture in another, and the panko in the third. Dip the lemon slices in the flour, then egg, then bread crumbs.

In a large skillet, heat the oil over medium heat. Add the lemon slices and cook for 2 minutes per side, or until golden brown and tender. Sprinkle with the salt and serve the fennel and lemon slices hot.

Notes

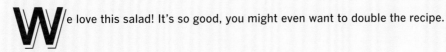

SERVES 4

We love this salad! It's so good, you might even want to double the recipe.

1 pound Brussels sprouts, ends trimmed, halved lengthwise

3 ounces thick-cut smoky bacon, cut crosswise into ½-inch strips

1 tablespoon extra-virgin olive oil

½ teaspoon coarse (kosher) salt

¼ teaspoon freshly ground black pepper

¼ cup mayonnaise

2 tablespoons red wine vinegar

2 teaspoons sugar

2 tablespoons finely chopped red onion or shallot

¼ cup raisins or dried currants

TIDBIT: *Brussels sprouts are often cheaper if you buy them on the stalk because of the labor involved in plucking the buds off. They also last significantly longer on the stalk (when kept in the fridge).*

Preheat the oven to 400°F.

In a large pot of boiling water, cook the Brussels sprouts for 5 minutes to parcook. Drain well.

Place the bacon and the sprouts in a small roasting pan and sprinkle with the oil, salt, and pepper. Roast for 35 minutes, or until the bacon is crisp and the sprouts are very tender.

Meanwhile, in a large bowl, whisk together the mayonnaise, vinegar, sugar, red onion, and raisins.

Add the Brussels sprouts, bacon, and any pan drippings to the dressing and toss to combine. Refrigerate until ready to serve.

Notes —————————————————

BUTTERNUT SQUASH CROSTINI WITH RAISINS AND BROWN BUTTER

For some reason, people are afraid of using butternut squash in anything but the classic soup. But like all winter squash, it's amazingly versatile. Here it makes for a perfect light meal or snack.

CROSTINI

30 thin slices (¼ inch) baguette (about ½ baguette, 4 to 5 ounces)

⅓ cup olive oil

2 garlic cloves, peeled and halved

1 teaspoon coarse (kosher) salt

TOPPING

1 pound butternut squash, halved, seeded, peeled, and cut crosswise into ½-inch-thick slices

3 shallots, thinly sliced

2 garlic cloves, skin on

2 tablespoons olive oil

2 tablespoons unsalted butter

2 teaspoons Dijon mustard

½ teaspoon coarse (kosher) salt

½ teaspoon freshly ground black pepper

2 tablespoons raisins or dried currants

To make the crostini: Preheat the oven to 350°F.

Place the slices of baguette on a large rimmed baking sheet and brush both sides with the oil. Bake for 10 to 12 minutes, turning the slices over midway, until golden brown and crisp. Remove from the oven (but leave the oven on and increase the temperature to 400°F). Rub the cut side of the garlic cloves over one side of each crostini. Sprinkle the salt over the top.

To make the topping: Arrange the squash, shallots, and garlic on a rimmed baking sheet and drizzle with the oil. Cover with foil and bake for 20 minutes. Uncover and bake for 15 minutes longer, or until the squash is very tender. Slip the skins off the garlic and transfer the garlic, squash, and shallots to a bowl.

In a small skillet, heat the butter over medium heat for 2 minutes, or until it foams, the foam subsides, and the butter starts to brown in spots. Add the butter to the same bowl along with mustard, salt, and pepper and gently mash until coarse. Stir in the raisins.

To serve, spoon about 2 teaspoons of the squash onto each crostini.

 Notes _____

VEGETABLE-CHEDDAR BREAKFAST MUFFINS

Once made and cooled, these can be individually wrapped in foil and frozen for a quick weekday breakfast or as a lunch box treat. To reheat, simply pop the still frozen wrapped muffin in a preheated 350°F oven for 10 to 15 minutes.

1 small zucchini (4 ounces)

2 cups all-purpose flour (spooned into cup and leveled off)

¼ cup sugar

2½ teaspoons baking powder

½ teaspoon baking soda

½ teaspoon salt

½ cup olive oil

1 large egg

1 cup buttermilk

1 cup shredded sharp Cheddar cheese (4 ounces)

1 small red bell pepper, cut into ¼-inch dice

Preheat the oven to 375°F. Line 12 cups of a muffin tin with paper liners.

Grate the zucchini on the large holes of a box grater. Transfer the zucchini to a fine-mesh sieve set over the sink, and with your hands, squeeze the zucchini as dry as possible.

In a large bowl, whisk together the flour, sugar, baking powder, baking soda, and salt.

In a separate bowl, whisk together the oil, egg, and buttermilk. Gently fold the flour mixture into the liquid. Fold in the Cheddar, zucchini, and bell pepper.

Divide the batter among the muffin cups (this is easily done using a ¼-cup ice cream scoop). Bake for 25 to 30 minutes, or until a wooden pick inserted in the center of a muffin comes out dry. Cool in the tin on a wire rack.

Notes

GINGERED CARROT PIE

Carrots get a double dose of ginger from both fresh and ground in this pie, which will remind you of pumpkin pie. Cooking the carrots first with a little sugar enhances their natural sweetness, and the fresh ginger gives them a little spicy kick.

DOUGH

1¼ cups all-purpose flour (spooned into cup and leveled off), plus more for rolling

1 tablespoon granulated sugar

¼ teaspoon salt

8 tablespoons (1 stick) cold unsalted butter, cut into bits

3 to 4 tablespoons ice water

FILLING

¾ pound carrots, thinly sliced

¼ cup plus 2 tablespoons granulated sugar

2 inches fresh ginger, thinly sliced

1 teaspoon ground cinnamon

2 large eggs

½ cup packed light brown sugar

2 tablespoons all-purpose flour

½ teaspoon ground ginger

1¼ cups half-and-half

To make the dough: In a large bowl, whisk together the flour, sugar, and salt. With a pastry blender or 2 knives used scissor-fashion, cut in the butter until large pea-size bits are formed. Add just enough of the ice water so the mixture holds together when pinched. Shape into a disk, wrap in plastic wrap, and refrigerate for 1 hour or up to 2 days.

On a lightly floured work surface, roll out the dough to a 12-inch round. Roll the dough around the rolling pin and fit it into a 9-inch pie plate without stretching it. Press the dough into the bottom and sides of the pan. With a pair of scissors, trim the dough to leave a 1-inch overhang all around. Fold the overhang in over the rim and, with your fingers, crimp the dough all around. Refrigerate at least 1 hour (this helps relax the dough so it doesn't shrink when baking).

Position the rack in the lower third of the oven and preheat to 400°F.

Prick the pie shell in several places. Line the pie shell with foil, leaving an overhang, and fill with pie weights to weight the crust down. Bake for 10 minutes, until the sides start to set. Remove the foil and weights and bake 5 minutes longer, or until the crust is golden brown but not completely cooked. Remove the pie crust but leave the oven on and reduce the temperature to 350°F.

To make the filling: In a medium saucepan, combine the carrots, 2 tablespoons of the granulated sugar, the fresh ginger, cinnamon, and water to cover by 2 inches and bring to a boil. Reduce to a simmer and cook 15 minutes, or until the carrots are very tender. Drain, transfer to a food processor, and puree until smooth. Add the eggs, the remaining ¼ cup granulated sugar, the brown sugar, flour, ground ginger, and half-and-half and pulse until well combined. Pour the mixture into the pie crust and bake until just set (the center may be slightly wobbly). Cool before serving.

Notes ———————————————

_____

_____

MUSHROOM, FONTINA, AND SPINACH PANINI

Panini are sandwiches that have been pressed and heated. Here we use one skillet on top of another to press the sandwich down. If you've got a panini press or a countertop hinged electric grill, use it instead. The Fontina and shiitakes in these panini make a winning combo.

2 tablespoons olive oil

6 ounces fresh shiitake mushrooms, stems discarded, caps thickly sliced

½ teaspoon coarse (kosher) salt

2 oval ciabatta rolls (each about 8 inches long)

2 tablespoons grainy mustard

4 ounces Fontina cheese (preferably Italian), thinly sliced

2 cups baby spinach

In a large skillet, heat 1 tablespoon of the oil over medium-low heat. Add the mushrooms, sprinkle with the salt, and cook for 5 to 7 minutes, stirring occasionally, until tender.

Split the ciabattas in half horizontally and spread with the mustard. Top with the Fontina, mushrooms, and spinach and close the sandwiches.

In a large skillet, heat the remaining 1 tablespoon oil over medium-low heat. Add the sandwiches and place another skillet on top of them. Place a few cans in the top skillet to weight it down and press. Cook for 2 to 3 minutes, lift the weights and skillet off, turn the sandwiches over, and repeat the pressing for another 2 to 3 minutes, or until the bread is crisp and the cheese has melted. Serve the panini hot.

Notes ————————————————

————————————————

————————————————

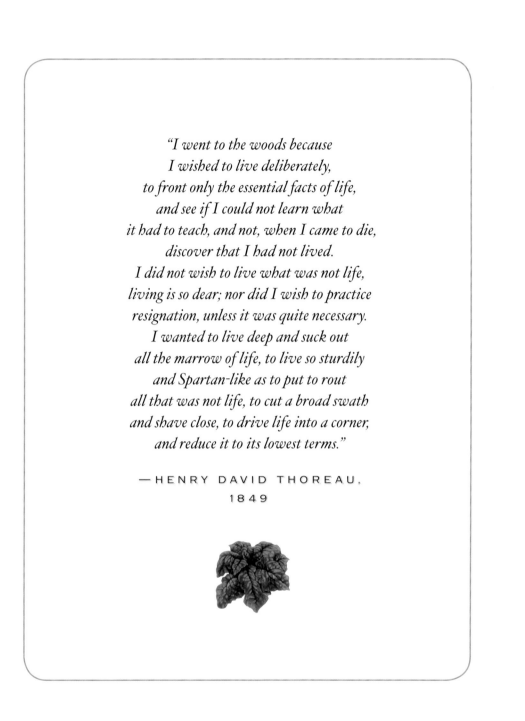

> *"I went to the woods because*
> *I wished to live deliberately,*
> *to front only the essential facts of life,*
> *and see if I could not learn what*
> *it had to teach, and not, when I came to die,*
> *discover that I had not lived.*
> *I did not wish to live what was not life,*
> *living is so dear; nor did I wish to practice*
> *resignation, unless it was quite necessary.*
> *I wanted to live deep and suck out*
> *all the marrow of life, to live so sturdily*
> *and Spartan-like as to put to rout*
> *all that was not life, to cut a broad swath*
> *and shave close, to drive life into a corner,*
> *and reduce it to its lowest terms."*

— HENRY DAVID THOREAU,
1849

FALL
RECIPES
FROM YOUR
FAMILY

Winter

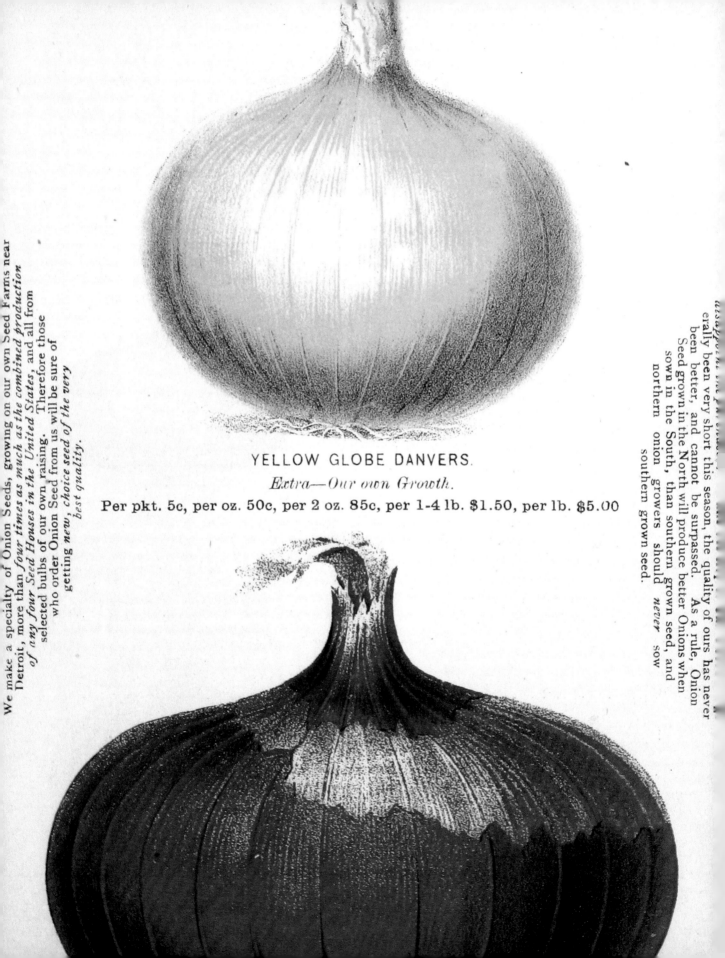

YELLOW GLOBE DANVERS.

Extra—Our own Growth.

Per pkt. 5c, per oz. 50c, per 2 oz. 85c, per 1-4 lb. $1.50, per lb. $5.00

We make a specialty of Onion Seeds, growing on our own Seed Farms near Detroit, more than *four times as much* as the combined production of any *four* Seed Houses *in the United States*, and all from selected bulbs of our own raising. Therefore those who order Onion Seed from us will be sure of getting *new, choice seed of the very best quality.*

erally been very short this season, the quality of ours has never been better, and cannot be surpassed. As a rule, Onion Seed grown in the North will produce better Onions when sown in the South, than southern grown seed, and northern onion growers should *never* sow southern grown seed.

Winter

"The greatest fine art of the future will be the making of a comfortable living from a small piece of land."

— ABRAHAM LINCOLN

BLAAK ONION JAM CHUTNEY

This chutney is perfect alongside a frittata or a plate of fried eggs, or with roasted, grilled, or broiled meats or poultry.

1 red bell pepper, cut into ½-inch squares

¾ cup chopped canned tomatoes

⅓ cup Blaak Onion Jam (see Tidbit)

1 tablespoon cider vinegar

1 tablespoon honey

2 tablespoons dried currants

¼ teaspoon coarse (kosher) salt

TIDBIT: *Blaak Onion Jam was the first condiment we ever created to pair with our famous Blaak cheese, but it's very versatile. It's made by caramelizing onions and then reducing them down in a mixture of maple syrup and balsamic vinegar. You can buy Blaak Onion Jam online at beekman1802.com; you'll also find the recipe there, so you can make it yourself.*

In a small saucepan or skillet, combine the bell pepper, tomatoes, onion jam, vinegar, and honey and bring to a simmer over low heat. Add the currants and salt, cover, and simmer for 10 minutes, or until the pepper is tender.

Uncover, increase the heat to medium, and cook for 3 minutes, or until most of the liquid has been absorbed and the chutney is thick.

Notes _____

WINTER SQUASH STUFFED WITH RED QUINOA

Acorn squash have sweet, slightly fibrous flesh and make a perfect container for quinoa. We like red quinoa as we find its flavor to be more interesting than regular quinoa. Here it's cooked in tea to give it even more depth to complement the sweetness of the squash. And the skin of acorn squash is edible, so you can eat the whole deal.

2 acorn squash (1½ pounds each), halved lengthwise and seeds discarded

2 tablespoons olive oil

1 tablespoon plus 1 teaspoon brown sugar

1½ teaspoons coarse (kosher) salt

½ teaspoon freshly ground black pepper

1 Irish or English breakfast tea bag

3 scallions, thinly sliced

2 garlic cloves, thinly sliced

1 cup red quinoa, rinsed

¼ teaspoon dried thyme

2 tablespoons unsalted butter

½ cup pecans, coarsely chopped

TIDBIT: *To make the raw acorn squash easier to halve, pierce the skin in a few spots then microwave on high for 2 minutes. Let stand for another few minutes before cutting.*

Preheat the oven to 450°F.

Cut a thin sliver from the uncut bottoms of each squash half (this is so they'll stand flat). Place the squash halves, cavity side up, on a rimmed baking sheet and brush the cavity with 1 tablespoon of the oil. Sprinkle the cavities with the brown sugar, ¾ teaspoon of the salt, and the pepper. Bake for 30 minutes, or until almost fork-tender.

Meanwhile, in a medium saucepan, bring 2 cups of water to a boil. Remove from the heat, add the tea bag, and steep for 3 minutes. Discard the tea bag.

In another medium saucepan, heat the remaining 1 tablespoon oil over medium heat. Add the scallions and garlic and cook for 2 minutes, stirring occasionally, until tender. Add the quinoa, the brewed tea, thyme, and the remaining ¾ teaspoon salt and bring to a boil. Reduce to a simmer, cover, and cook for 17 minutes, or until the quinoa is tender and the liquid has been absorbed. Stir in the butter and pecans.

Divide the quinoa among the squash halves, tent loosely with foil, and bake for 30 minutes, or until the squash is very tender.

Notes ————————————————

CORNFLAKE-CRUMBED ONION RINGS

Onion rings get extra crispy when coated with crushed cornflakes. Don't be afraid of deep-frying: If the oil is at the right temperature, it won't get absorbed by the onions. (If you don't believe us, measure the oil after you've cooked the onions.)

1 large onion (8 to 10 ounces),
 peeled

1 cup all-purpose flour (spooned
 into cup and leveled off)

1 teaspoon baking powder

½ cup whole milk

1 large egg

1 cup cornflake crumbs (from about
 2 cups cornflakes or Special K
 cereal)

Vegetable oil, for deep-frying

Coarse (kosher) salt

TIDBIT: *To get rid of "onion breath,"*
eat a sprig or two of parsley dipped in
vinegar or salt. You can also chew on
fennel seeds or coffee beans.

Cut the onion into ½-inch-thick rounds. Soak in a bowl of cold water for 10 minutes, then drain well and pat dry.

Set up 3 shallow bowls. Stir together the flour and baking powder in one. Whisk together the milk and egg in another. Put the cornflake crumbs in the third. Dip the onion into the flour mixture, shaking off the excess. Dip the flour-coated onion into the egg mixture, letting the excess drip off. Dip the onion into the cornflake crumbs and place on a wire rack while you heat the oil.

In a deep saucepan, pour in oil to come up 2 inches. Heat the oil over medium heat to 350°F on a deep-frying thermometer. (Alternatively, if you don't have a thermometer, drop a little flour into the oil; if it sizzles, the oil is ready.)

Working in batches, so you don't crowd the onions (which would bring the temperature in the saucepan down), fry for 2 to 3 minutes, or until golden brown and crisp. Transfer to a plate lined with paper towels and repeat with the remaining onions. Sprinkle with salt and serve hot.

Notes _____

_____

_____

ROASTED BROCCOLI WITH HOT PEPPER FLAKES

We love roasting broccoli until it lightly browns and crisps, and then serve it with a creamy Italian dipping sauce called *bagna cauda*, which translates as "hot bath." The bath here is made of cream with some cream cheese to thicken, and anchovies that melt down and give the sauce deep flavor. If you've had anchovies on a pizza and are ready to say "no thank you," we think you should try this; you'll be surprised at how good they can be (and you won't even notice they're there).

1 bunch broccoli (1¼ pounds)

4 tablespoons olive oil

½ teaspoon coarse (kosher) salt

4 garlic cloves, finely chopped

6 anchovy fillets, mashed

¾ cup heavy cream

4 tablespoons cream cheese

½ teaspoon red pepper flakes

TIDBIT: *Broccoli that is overmature becomes woody because its sugars are converted to lignin, a type of fiber that will not soften with cooking.*

Preheat the oven to 450°F.

Trim the very end of the broccoli stalks, then cut the stalks lengthwise with the florets attached into long pieces. Place on a rimmed baking sheet and drizzle with 3 tablespoons of the oil. Sprinkle with the salt and toss to coat. Roast for 20 minutes, turning the broccoli, until it is browned.

Meanwhile, in a small saucepan, heat the remaining 1 tablespoon oil over low heat. Add the garlic and anchovies and cook for 2 minutes, stirring occasionally, until the anchovies melt. Add the cream, cream cheese, and pepper flakes. Increase the heat to medium and bring to a boil. Cook, stirring occasionally, for 3 to 5 minutes, until the sauce is lightly thickened and reduced to ¾ cup.

Serve the broccoli with the warm sauce for dipping.

Notes

GROWN-UP ANTS ON A LOG

MAKES 12 PIECES

This grown-up take on a childhood treat would make a perfect party starter. Ancho chile powder, spicy and smoky, can be found on the supermarket spice shelf.

¼ cup dried currants

2 tablespoons Scotch whiskey

1 log (4 ounces) soft goat cheese

2 tablespoons mango chutney, finely chopped

2 teaspoons Dijon mustard

½ teaspoon ancho chile powder

¼ teaspoon coarse (kosher) salt

4 celery stalks, cut into 3-inch lengths

¼ cup pecans, toasted and coarsely chopped

TIDBIT: *Celery was first introduced to America in 1856 when a Scotsman named George Taylor brought celery to Kalamazoo, Michigan. By 1872 farmers were transforming acres of Michigan mucklands into celery fields. Kalamazoo began promoting itself as the Celery City and became known around the country for the "strange" vegetable.*

In a small bowl, combine the currants and Scotch and let stand for 30 minutes, or until the currants have softened and absorbed the Scotch.

In another small bowl, with an electric mixer, beat the goat cheese until smooth. Beat in the chutney, mustard, ancho powder, and salt.

Fit a pastry bag with a decorative tip and fill with the cheese mixture. Pipe the cheese mixture into the celery. (Alternatively, use a spoon to fill the celery.) Sprinkle the pecans and currants over the top, pressing them in to adhere.

 *Notes* _____

ITALIAN-STYLE STUFFED CABBAGE

As the Tidbit below suggests, this recipe is fit for a king. We especially like soft, tender Savoy cabbage for this dish, but when it isn't in season, you can use regular green cabbage or large escarole leaves. The Italian sausage and Parmesan cheese give this its decidedly Italian flair. The technique of using custard cups or ramekins to form the stuffed cabbage bundles, rather than simply rolling the leaves around the stuffing, makes the bundles neater and more even.

2 tablespoons olive oil

1 onion, finely chopped

3 garlic cloves, thinly sliced

1 can (28 ounces) diced fire-roasted tomatoes

8 large Savoy cabbage leaves, from a large head

1 pound sweet or hot Italian sausage, casings removed

¹/₂ cup grated Parmesan cheese

¹/₃ cup panko bread crumbs

¹/₃ cup whole milk

TIDBIT: *Russian princes paid tributes not only with racing horses and jewels, but also with garden plots planted with* kapusta—*Russian (and Polish) for cabbage.*

Preheat the oven to 350°F.

In a large ovenproof skillet, heat the oil over medium heat. Add the onion and garlic and cook for 7 to 10 minutes, stirring occasionally, until the onion is tender. Transfer to a large bowl and cool to room temperature.

Add the tomatoes to the skillet and bring to a boil over medium heat. Reduce to a simmer and cook for 5 minutes to reduce slightly. Set aside.

Meanwhile, bring a large pot of water to a boil and set up a bowl with ice and water. Cut off the thick ribs of the cabbage, trimming them even with the bottoms of the cabbage leaves. Blanch the cabbage leaves in the boiling water for 15 seconds to soften and make them more pliable. Lift the leaves out of the water and transfer to the bowl of ice water to stop the cooking. Drain and pat the leaves dry.

Add the sausage, Parmesan, panko, and milk to the onion mixture and use your hands to mix until combined. Place a cabbage leaf in each of four 6-ounce custard cups or ramekins, overlapping the leaves where the rib portions were removed so there are no holes and leaving an overhang (this happens naturally as the leaves are larger than the cup). Divide half of the sausage mixture among the 4 leaves, fold the overhang over the mixture to cover, and transfer them, seam-side down, to the skillet with the tomatoes. Repeat with the remaining 4 cabbage leaves and the remaining sausage mixture.

Bring to a simmer over medium heat, cover, and bake for 30 minutes, or until the cabbages feel firm to the touch.

Serve 2 of the cabbages per person with the tomato sauce spooned over.

Notes ——————————————————————

DATE AND WINTER SQUASH SALAD WITH PISTACHIOS

SERVES 4

Sweet acorn squash seems to get even sweeter once it's been roasted. And we love the fact that there's no need to peel the skin of an acorn squash; it becomes tender and edible when cooked. A tart-sweet dressing seasoned with a hot Indian spice blend called garam masala heightens the flavor of the salad. Look for garam masala in the spice section of the supermarket.

1 acorn squash (about 1½ pounds), well washed

2 tablespoons olive oil

1 tablespoon sugar

1 teaspoon coarse (kosher) salt

¼ cup fresh lime juice

2 tablespoons red currant jelly or apricot jam, melted

½ teaspoon garam masala

¼ teaspoon freshly ground black pepper

1 cup dates, pitted and cut crosswise into ½-inch pieces

½ cup pistachios

6 cups torn leaf lettuce

TIDBIT: *Winter squash will last several months in a cool (50° to 55°F), dark cellar or storage area, but only about 2 weeks in the refrigerator. Ideally, only cut or cooked acorn squash should be refrigerated.*

Preheat the oven to 450°F. Line a rimmed baking sheet with foil (for easier cleanup).

Halve the squash lengthwise, then scrape out and discard the seeds. Halve the squash lengthwise again and then slice each quarter crosswise into ½-inch-thick slices.

Place the squash on the baking sheet, drizzle with the oil, sprinkle with the sugar and ½ teaspoon of the salt, and toss to coat. Roast for 30 minutes, or until the squash is tender.

Meanwhile, in a large bowl, whisk together the lime juice, jelly, garam masala, pepper, and the remaining ½ teaspoon salt.

Add the squash, dates, pistachios, and lettuce to the dressing and toss to combine. Divide among 4 plates and serve.

Notes ———

OKONOMIYAKI WITH SHRIMP (JAPANESE PANCAKE)

SERVES 4

*O*konomiyaki translates to "as you like it" in Japanese, meaning you can put whatever you have available into this savory pancake. Cabbage seems to be necessary, but after that you can be as creative as you like. While it often contains squid, we've used shrimp—but hey, if you'd rather use something like chicken, go ahead.

1 tablespoon vegetable oil

4 slices bacon, quartered crosswise

½ cup all-purpose flour

1 teaspoon baking powder

½ teaspoon coarse (kosher) salt

2 large eggs

1 tablespoon soy sauce

2 cups finely shredded green cabbage (6 ounces)

1 carrot, peeled with a vegetable peeler into ribbons (1 cup)

3 tablespoons finely chopped fresh ginger

3 scallions, thinly sliced

½ pound shrimp, peeled, deveined, and coarsely chopped

3 tablespoons ketchup

2 teaspoons Worcestershire sauce

1 teaspoon honey

2 tablespoons mayonnaise

TIDBIT: *Baseball legend Babe Ruth used to wear a cabbage leaf on his head beneath his ball cap.*

In a large cast-iron or nonstick skillet, heat the oil over medium-low heat. Add 4 of the bacon pieces and cook for 7 to 10 minutes, or until crisp. Lift the bacon out of the pan, leaving the grease in the pan.

Meanwhile, in a large bowl, whisk together the flour, baking powder, salt, eggs, and soy sauce until well combined. Fold in the cabbage, carrot, ginger, scallions, and shrimp. Crumble in the cooked bacon.

Place the remaining 12 pieces of bacon in the skillet in 4 clusters of 3 pieces each and heat over medium heat. Using a ½-cup measuring cup, scoop the batter onto each pile of bacon and flatten each to about a 4-inch round. Cook until the pancakes are set and golden brown on the underside, and the bacon is crisp. Flip the pancakes over and cook for 3 to 5 minutes longer, or until cooked through.

In a small bowl, stir together the ketchup, Worcestershire, and honey. Dollop 1½ teaspoons of mayonnaise on top of each pancake and drizzle the ketchup mixture on top. Serve hot.

Notes _____

_____

_____

ROASTED RUTABAGA WITH A GUINNESS GLAZE

uinness, a dry Irish stout, gives the already slightly peppery rutabaga a mildly bitter edge that's tamed by the addition of brown sugar. As the rutabaga cooks, the Guinness evaporates and the olive oil gives the turnip a glossy finish. You'll find lots of large waxed rutabagas in the market, but search out the smaller, unwaxed oncs for the sweetest flavor.

$^3/_4$ cup Guinness stout

3 tablespoons olive oil

2 tablespoons light brown sugar

$^1/_2$ teaspoon coarse (kosher) salt

$^1/_4$ teaspoon freshly ground black pepper

2 pounds small unwaxed rutabagas, peeled and cut into 1-inch chunks

TIDBIT: *Legend has it that a black-smith named Jack found his way through the underworld using a large, hollowed-out rutabaga with glowing coal inside. This tale was the origin of the modern-day jack-o'-lantern.*

Preheat the oven to 400°F.

In a large bowl, whisk together the Guinness, oil, brown sugar, salt, and pepper. Add the rutabaga and toss to coat.

Transfer to a 9 × 13-inch baking pan and roast for 50 minutes, tossing occasionally, until tender. Serve warm.

Notes ———

DOUBLE CREAM OF CELERY SOUP

Celery and celery root combine to make this a double celery soup. Just a small amount of cream is needed to make it extra creamy. If you've got a bunch of celery with their leaves, you can use the leaves to garnish the soup.

4 tablespoons unsalted butter

6 pale-green celery stalks, thinly sliced (3 cups)

1 medium celery root (celeriac), peeled and thinly sliced (1 cup)

1 medium onion, thinly sliced

1 medium russet (baking) potato, peeled and thinly sliced

½ teaspoon coarse (kosher) salt, plus more to taste

3 cups chicken broth

½ teaspoon fresh lemon or regular thyme leaves

¼ cup heavy cream

TIDBIT: *Also known as celeriac, this rough globular swollen root is often muddied, gnarled, and full of wild offshoot stubbles. Underneath the root's burly exterior, though, is a bright white flesh with a crisp, apple-like texture. The firm flesh has a mild herbaceous quality with celery-like undertones.*

In a medium saucepan, melt the butter over medium-low heat. Add the celery, celery root, onion, and potato and sprinkle with the salt. Cover and cook for 25 minutes, stirring occasionally, until the vegetables are tender but not browned.

Add the broth and thyme and bring to a simmer. Cook for 15 minutes, or until the vegetables are almost falling apart.

Working in batches, transfer to a blender, add the cream, and puree until very smooth. Season to taste with more salt, if you like, and serve hot.

Notes

SWEET AND SOUR SHALLOTS

SERVES 4

Serve these alongside a steak or roasted chicken. They're sweet and tangy from the vinegar and sugar, and buttery from long, slow cooking in a butter-oil combo. We used a Sauvignon Blanc vinegar from KATZ in California for its deep flavor, but you can swap in cider vinegar. Though commercially available at supermarkets, you will also find this vinegar at apple orchard farm stands.

1 tablespoon unsalted butter

1 tablespoon olive oil

1 pound shallots (about 20), peeled

1½ inches fresh ginger, thinly sliced
  (no need to peel)

2 sprigs fresh lemon thyme or
  regular thyme

4 teaspoons sugar

2 tablespoons Sauvignon Blanc
  vinegar

½ teaspoon coarse (kosher) salt

In a medium skillet, heat the butter and oil over medium-low heat. Add the shallots, ginger, and thyme and cook for 20 minutes, shaking the pan occasionally, until the shallots are buttery, richly browned, and almost tender.

Add the sugar and cook for 2 minutes, or until melted. Add the vinegar and salt and cook for 3 to 5 minutes, shaking the pan frequently, until the shallots are nicely coated and the sauce is syrupy. Serve hot or at room temperature.

Notes _____

_____

_____

SAVORY VEGETABLE BREAD PUDDING

Sweet onions and mushrooms combine with bread in a savory side dish that's reminiscent of French onion soup.

2 tablespoons olive oil, plus more for the baking dish

1 tablespoon unsalted butter

3 large sweet onions (such as Vidalia or Maui) or Spanish onions, halved and thinly sliced (6 cups)

1/2 pound mushrooms, thinly sliced

3 large eggs

2 cups whole milk

1 cup heavy cream

1 1/2 teaspoons coarse (kosher) salt

1/2 teaspoon freshly ground black pepper

1/2 teaspoon crumbled dried sage

1 baguette (8 ounces), halved lengthwise and cut crosswise into 1-inch pieces

8 ounces Fontina cheese (preferably Italian), cut into 1-inch cubes

TIDBIT: *Storage onions are low in water and high in sulfur, so they store well and are available year-round. Storage onions are more pungent and flavorful than sweet onions, and they're best if cooked.*

In a large, deep skillet, heat the oil and butter over medium heat. Add the onions and cook for 35 minutes, stirring occasionally, until golden brown and soft. Add the mushrooms and cook for 5 to 7 minutes, or until the mushrooms are tender.

Preheat the oven to 350°F. Brush a 9 × 13-inch baking dish with oil.

In a large bowl, whisk together the eggs, milk, cream, salt, pepper, and sage. Add the bread, the onion mixture, and Fontina and stir to combine.

Pour the mixture into the baking dish, pressing so the bread is covered with liquid, and set aside to soak for at least 10 minutes, until the bread has absorbed most of the liquid.

Bake for 35 minutes, or until the bread is crisp and the custard is set. Serve hot or at room temperature.

Notes _____

CELERY ROOT AND POTATO GRATIN

Celery root and potatoes have a natural affinity for each other, and Gruyère, a nutty Swiss cheese, marries the two together.

1 garlic clove, peeled and halved

Softened butter, for the baking dish

1½ cups heavy cream

1 cup whole milk

½ teaspoon grated lemon zest

¼ teaspoon chopped fresh rosemary

¾ teaspoon coarse (kosher) salt

¼ teaspoon freshly ground black pepper

1¼ pounds celery root (celeriac), peeled and thinly sliced (see Tidbit)

1¼ pounds russet (baking) potatoes, peeled and thinly sliced

1½ cups shredded Gruyère, Gouda, or Fontina cheese (6 ounces)

TIDBIT: *If you've peeled the celery root in advance, you can toss it in a bowl of acidulated water (water that's had either a little lemon juice or vinegar added to it) to preserve its bright white color.*

Preheat the oven to 375°F. Rub a 9 × 13-inch baking dish with the cut sides of the garlic and brush with butter.

In a medium saucepan, combine the cream, milk, lemon zest, rosemary, salt, and pepper and bring to a simmer over medium heat.

Transfer the hot cream mixture to a bowl and add the celery root and potatoes tossing well to coat, separating them so all sides are coated.

Scoop half the mixture into the baking dish and press down with your hands. Scatter half the Gruyère on top. Top with the remaining vegetables, pressing down to pack them in, and pour the cream mixture remaining in the bowl over the top. Sprinkle with the remaining Gruyère.

Bake for 1 hour 30 minutes, or until the celery root and potatoes are fork-tender and the top is browned. Serve warm.

Notes

THE BEEKMAN 1802 STUFFED PEPPERS

We've reinvented the stuffed pepper and given it a Spanish touch, with chorizo and smoked paprika. If you'd like to gild the lily here, once you've spooned the pasta mixture into the peppers, sprinkle the tops with shredded Manchego cheese and bake just until the cheese has melted.

4 bell peppers, mixed colors

4 tablespoons olive oil

1 small red onion, finely chopped ($\frac{1}{2}$ cup)

2 garlic cloves, thinly sliced

3 ounces (1 small link) dried chorizo, quartered lengthwise and thinly sliced crosswise

$\frac{3}{4}$ cup small star-shaped pasta (stelline) or orzo

2 plum tomatoes, diced

1 cup water

$\frac{1}{2}$ teaspoon coarse (kosher) salt

$\frac{1}{2}$ teaspoon sweet smoked paprika

Preheat the oven to 450°F.

Remove $\frac{1}{4}$ inch of the tops of the peppers. Discard the stems and finely chop the pepper tops. Halve the peppers lengthwise, and scoop out and discard the seeds. Drizzle the pepper halves inside and out with 2 tablespoons of the oil and place them cut-side down on a rimmed baking sheet. Bake for 20 minutes, or until crisp-tender. If you like, remove the pepper skins.

Meanwhile, in a medium saucepan, heat the remaining 2 tablespoons oil over medium heat. Add the onion, garlic, and chopped pepper tops and cook for 7 minutes, stirring occasionally, until tender. Stir in the chorizo, pasta, tomatoes, water, salt, and smoked paprika and bring to a boil. Reduce to a simmer and cook for 10 minutes, or until the pasta is al dente.

Spoon the mixture into the pepper halves and serve.

Notes _____

_____

_____

GOLDEN CRISPY RICE WITH WINTER VEGETABLES

Buttery, crispy rice studded with vegetables—just the way we like it. For the best flavor and texture, use one of the aromatic long-grain rices, such as jasmine or Texmati. They're fragrant, and the grains cook up separate and fluffy.

5 tablespoons unsalted butter

2 cups cooked long-grain rice

⅓ cup whole milk

¾ teaspoon coarse (kosher) salt

1 small onion, finely chopped

1 cup cut green beans (½-inch lengths), stem ends trimmed

1 cup shredded carrots

2 garlic cloves, thinly sliced

In a large cast-iron or heavy-bottom skillet, heat 3 tablespoons of the butter over medium-low heat. Add the rice, milk, and salt and press into an even layer. Cook for 15 minutes, without stirring, until the bottom is crispy.

Turn the rice over in the skillet, add another tablespoon of the butter to the rice and cook for 10 to 15 minutes, without stirring, until the underside is crispy.

Make a well in the center of the rice, pushing the rice to the edges of the skillet. Add the remaining 1 tablespoon butter to the well along with the onion, green beans, carrots, and garlic. Cook for 5 to 7 minutes, stirring the vegetables and rice frequently, until tender.

Serve the rice and vegetables warm, directly from the pan, making sure each diner gets some of the crispy bits.

Notes

YUKON GOLD POTATO SALAD

Butter-yellow Yukon Gold potatoes have a creamy texture. We call for small ones and cook them whole so they don't become waterlogged.

2 large eggs

2½ pounds small Yukon Gold potatoes, well scrubbed

1 teaspoon coarse (kosher) salt

⅓ cup mayonnaise

⅓ cup sour cream

¼ teaspoon freshly ground black pepper

½ cup finely chopped red onion

1 celery stalk, quartered lengthwise and thinly sliced

TIDBIT: *The potato was not popular in the United States until the middle of the 19th century. Before that, many people thought that the tubers were poisonous and others did not like the yellowish color of the flesh. In 1811, the Landreth Seed Company introduced a potato with a white flesh, and this potato gradually gained acceptance. Today all sorts of potatoes are popular (including purple and blue), but the once-shunned yellow potato is now among the most well loved.*

In a small saucepan, cover the eggs with cold water. Bring to a boil over high heat, remove from the heat, cover, and let stand for 12 minutes. Drain, lightly crack the shells, and transfer to a bowl of ice water. Let stand for 10 minutes, then peel and coarsely chop.

Place the potatoes in a large pot of water, add ¼ teaspoon of the salt, and bring to a boil. Reduce to a simmer and cook for 25 minutes, or until the potatoes are tender enough to pierce with a knife, but not falling apart (timing will vary depending on the size of the potatoes). When cool enough to handle, peel and cut into ½-inch-thick rounds.

Meanwhile, in a large bowl, stir together the mayonnaise, sour cream, pepper, and the remaining ¾ teaspoon salt. Add the onion, celery, chopped eggs, and potatoes and stir gently to combine.

Notes

BEEKMAN 1802 SPLIT PEA SOUP

Sometimes it is hard to put a twist on something as classic and perfect as pea soup, but we always try to keep things interesting. You can use green or yellow split peas for this earthy, Indian-spiced soup.

3 tablespoons olive oil

1 medium onion, finely chopped

3 garlic cloves, thinly sliced

2 teaspoons ground cumin

2 teaspoons ground coriander

1½ teaspoons ground ginger

1 carrot, thinly sliced

½ pound yellow squash, halved lengthwise and cut crosswise into ½-inch-thick slices

½ pound Yukon Gold potatoes, peeled, quartered, and cut into ½-inch-thick slices

¾ cup split peas

2 tablespoons tomato paste

6 cups water

1 teaspoon coarse (kosher) salt

TIDBIT: *A 100-calorie serving of split peas (about ½ cup) contains more protein than a whole egg or tablespoon of peanut butter.*

In a large saucepan, heat the oil over medium heat. Add the onion and garlic and cook for 7 minutes, stirring occasionally, until the onion is tender. Stir in the cumin, coriander, and ginger and cook for 1 minute.

Add the carrot, yellow squash, and potatoes and stir to combine. Stir in the split peas, tomato paste, water, and salt and bring to a boil. Reduce to a simmer, cover, and cook for 35 to 40 minutes, stirring occasionally, until the split peas are tender.

Notes _____

_____

_____

CACCIATORE À LA 1802

While chicken cacciatore is traditionally made with fresh mushrooms, our reinvented cacciatore uses dried porcini along with its soaking liquid and fire-roasted tomatoes with chiles for a spicy, earthy finish. Not all recipes call for capers, but we love the hit of brininess they add to the dish.

1/3 cup dried porcini

1 cup hot water

2 tablespoons olive oil

8 bone-in, skin-on chicken thighs (about 5 ounces each), skin removed (see Tidbit)

1/3 cup all-purpose flour

1 medium onion, diced

1 green bell pepper, diced

2 garlic cloves, thinly sliced

1/3 cup red wine

1 can (14.5 ounces) diced fire-roasted tomatoes with green chiles

1 tablespoon capers, rinsed

1/2 teaspoon crumbled dried rosemary

1/2 teaspoon coarse (kosher) salt

1/2 teaspoon freshly ground black pepper

TIDBIT: *There's no need to pay extra money for skinless chicken thighs; they're easy enough to skin yourself. Holding a paper towel in one hand and the chicken in the other, grab the skin with the paper towel and simply pull it off.*

In a small bowl, combine the porcini and hot water and let stand for 30 minutes at room temperature until the porcini have softened.

In a large skillet, heat 1 tablespoon of the oil over medium heat. Dredge the chicken in the flour, shaking off any excess. Add the chicken to the skillet and cook for 3 to 4 minutes per side, or until golden brown. Transfer to a bowl.

Add the remaining 1 tablespoon oil to the skillet. Add the onion, bell pepper, and garlic and cook for 10 minutes, stirring occasionally, until the onion is tender. Add the wine and bring to a boil.

Lift the porcini out of the water, rinse, and coarsely chop. Strain the soaking liquid through a fine-mesh sieve and add it to the skillet along with the porcini. Bring to a boil. Add the tomatoes, capers, rosemary, salt, and pepper and return to a boil.

Return the chicken to the skillet, reduce to a simmer, cover, and cook for 35 minutes, or until the chicken is cooked through and tender. Serve warm.

Notes _____

KALE SMOOTHIE

We know that kale is good for us, but you know what? It tastes good, too! Paired with banana and pineapple, this smoothie has a tropical feel.

1 cup chopped fresh kale leaves
   (1½ ounces)

1 small banana (5 ounces), sliced

½ cup plain whole-milk Greek
   yogurt

¾ cup pineapple juice

2 tablespoons honey

1 tablespoon fresh lemon juice

3 ice cubes

In a blender, combine the kale, banana, yogurt, pineapple juice, honey, lemon juice, and ice cubes and puree until thick and smooth.

Notes ——————————

ICEBERG BLT WEDGE WITH BLUE CHEESE CROUTONS

Think of this as an inside-out BLT with the added bonus of creamy blue cheese.

4 slices bacon

2 cups cubed (½-inch) French bread, without crusts (2 ounces)

2 tablespoons olive oil

2 ounces firm blue cheese, crumbled

⅔ cup mayonnaise

2 tablespoons fresh lemon juice

2 tablespoons tomato paste

½ teaspoon freshly ground black pepper

1 head iceberg lettuce, quartered lengthwise

1 large tomato, cut into large dice

Preheat the oven to 350°F.

Place the bacon in a single layer on a rimmed baking sheet and bake for 10 minutes, turning it once, until crisp. Transfer to a plate lined with paper towels and when cool enough to handle, break into large pieces. Pour 1 tablespoon of the bacon grease into a small bowl.

On a separate rimmed baking sheet, toss the bread cubes with the oil and blue cheese, and bake for 20 minutes, tossing occasionally, until the cubes are crisp.

To the bowl with the bacon grease, whisk in the mayonnaise, lemon juice, tomato paste, and pepper.

To serve, place the lettuce wedges on 4 plates. Drizzle with the mayonnaise mixture and scatter the blue cheese croutons, tomato, and bacon over the top.

 *Notes*

BACON-POPPED POPCORN

What household doesn't love a movie night? Smoky bacon with a fair amount of fat is cooked to crisp the bacon and render the fat. The popping corn is then cooked in the fat, giving it some smoky flavor. Have the popcorn as a snack, or use it as a garnish for Smoky Roasted Corn Soup (page 112).

1 tablespoon vegetable oil

4 slices bacon

¼ cup popping corn

Coarse (kosher) salt

In a small skillet, heat the oil over medium-low heat. Add the bacon and cook for 7 minutes, or until crisp. Transfer the bacon to a plate lined with paper towels. When cool enough to handle, coarsely crumble.

Transfer the bacon fat to a deep saucepan or stovetop popcorn popper and heat over medium-high heat. Place 2 popcorn kernels in the pan and when they pop, add the remaining kernels. Cover and cook, shaking the pan constantly, until the popcorn stops popping.

Immediately transfer to a bowl, add the crumbled bacon and salt to taste, and toss to coat.

Notes

VEGETABLE CREAM CHEESE

O n the rare occasions when we felt like rewarding ourselves while living in New York City, we'd spend Sunday mornings searching for the best "everything" bagel and the best veggie cream cheese to go along with it. But why buy it when it's so simple to make it yourself? This recipe is versatile: Don't like dill? Swap in cilantro or parsley. Chives can stand in for scallions (or omit them altogether). Play around and make it your own.

8 ounces (1 package) cream cheese,
   at room temperature

1/2 cup finely diced carrot

1/2 cup finely diced red bell pepper

1/4 cup thinly sliced scallion

1/4 cup finely diced celery

2 tablespoons minced fresh dill

1 teaspoon grated lemon zest

In a large bowl, lightly mash the cream cheese. Stir in the carrot, bell pepper, scallion, celery, dill, and lemon zest. Transfer to a lidded container and store in the refrigerator for up to 1 week.

Notes

SOUP STARTER

What is a soup starter, anyway? For us it's something called a *sofrito*, a mixture that Puerto Rican and Caribbean cooks keep on hand to start a soup (see Easy Bean Soup, below), bean dish, or stew, or to stir into cooked rice. We use it in place of the onions, garlic, and carrots that might be called for to start a dish. Once made, it'll keep in the fridge for up to a week or frozen for up to a year. We like to pack it in ice cube trays and use a couple of cubes when needed. Pop the cubes out of the trays and pack into zipseal bags—remember to label and date them.

½ cup olive oil

2 cups chopped onion

1 cup diced leeks

1 cup coarsely chopped carrot

5 finely chopped garlic cloves

1 red bell pepper, coarsely chopped

1 green bell pepper, coarsely chopped

2 cups chopped canned or fresh tomatoes

1 teaspoon fresh thyme leaves

1 teaspoon coarse (kosher) salt

In a medium saucepan, heat the oil over medium-low heat. Add the onion, leeks, carrot, garlic, and bell peppers and cook for 30 minutes, stirring frequently, until the vegetables are very soft and tender.

Add the tomatoes, thyme, and salt and cook for 10 to 15 minutes, stirring frequently, until the mixture is thick and glossy. Cool to room temperature, then refrigerate up to a week. For longer storage, freeze in portion-size containers or in ice cube trays.

Easy Bean Soup: Combine an assortment of dried beans to make 2 cups (try pinto, great Northern, navy, and black beans) and soak in cold water overnight. Drain. In a large pot, combine the beans, 1 cup of the soup starter, and 6 cups water and bring to a boil. Reduce to a simmer, cover, and cook, stirring occasionally, for 1 hour 30 minutes, or until the beans are tender. If necessary, add a little more water as the beans cook so the soup isn't too thick.

Notes _____

_____

_____

ROOT VEGETABLE HASH
WITH PANCETTA AND PECORINO

W e love hash, and it doesn't have to be the corned beef kind. A mix of root vegetables makes for a great side dish, but if you're like us, you'll want to top it with a fried egg for a perfect breakfast.

½ pound Yukon Gold potatoes, peeled and cut into 1-inch chunks

½ pound white turnip, peeled and cut into 1-inch chunks

½ pound parsnips, peeled and cut into ½-inch-thick slices

¾ pound kabocha or other winter squash, peeled and cut into 1-inch chunks

4 tablespoons olive oil

3 ounces pancetta or bacon, coarsely chopped

1 medium onion, coarsely chopped

1 teaspoon coarse (kosher) salt

½ teaspoon dried thyme

⅓ cup grated Pecorino Romano cheese

In a large pot of boiling water, cook the potatoes and turnip for 5 minutes. Add the parsnips and squash and cook for 3 minutes, or until all the vegetables are crisp-tender. Drain.

Meanwhile, in a large skillet, heat 2 tablespoons of the oil over medium heat. Add the pancetta and cook for 3 to 5 minutes, or until the pancetta is crisp. Add the onion and 1 tablespoon of the oil and cook for 5 to 7 minutes, stirring occasionally, or until the onion is glossy.

Add the remaining 1 tablespoon oil, the squash mixture, salt, and thyme and cook for 3 minutes, stirring occasionally. Press on the vegetables and cook for 5 minutes, without stirring, or until it starts to form a crust on the bottom. Scatter the pecorino over the mixture, turn the vegetables over (the cheese will be on the bottom), and cook for 3 to 5 minutes, without stirring, or until a crust forms on the bottom. Serve hot.

Notes

PASTA, BROCCOLI, AND TWO-CHEESE CASSEROLE

We've used Gouda, a semi-hard Dutch cheese, here for its nutty flavor. Look for imported Gouda, which is more full-flavored than its American cousin. And though we used regular Gouda, if you'd like, swap in a smoked Gouda for a slightly different flavor.

1 bunch broccoli (1¼ pounds)

¾ pound mezze rigatoni or other short tubular pasta

7 tablespoons unsalted butter

1 Granny Smith apple, peeled and coarsely chopped

3 tablespoons all-purpose flour

4 cups whole milk

1 teaspoon coarse (kosher) salt

½ teaspoon freshly ground black pepper

½ pound (once the wax rind is removed) Gouda cheese, shredded

1 cup grated Parmesan cheese

1 cup panko bread crumbs

TIDBIT: *The average person will consume more than 4 pounds of broccoli per year. We think you can do better than that.*

Preheat the oven to 350°F.

Separate the broccoli florets and the stalks. Trim the very end of the stalks and then, with a paring knife, peel the remaining stalk. Thinly slice the stalks and cut the florets into bite-size pieces.

In a large pot of boiling water, cook the pasta according to package directions, adding the broccoli to the pan during the final 2 minutes of cooking. Drain well.

Meanwhile, in a large saucepan, melt 4 tablespoons of the butter over medium heat. Add the apple and cook for 2 minutes, stirring occasionally, or until crisp-tender. Add the flour, stirring to coat. Gradually add the milk and stir for 3 to 5 minutes, or until lightly thickened. Stir in the salt and pepper and remove from the heat. Stir the Gouda and ¾ cup of the Parmesan into the sauce, stirring until the cheese has melted.

Add the cooked pasta and broccoli to the cheese sauce, stirring until well coated, and transfer to a 9 × 13-inch baking dish.

In a small skillet, melt the remaining 3 tablespoons butter over medium-low heat. Add the panko and cook for 2 to 3 minutes, stirring constantly, or until the panko is lightly crisp and golden.

Scatter the crumbs over the top of the pasta and sprinkle the remaining ¼ cup Parmesan over the top. Bake for 30 minutes, or until the pasta is piping hot and the topping is crisp. Let sit for 5 minutes before serving.

Notes _____

_____

_____

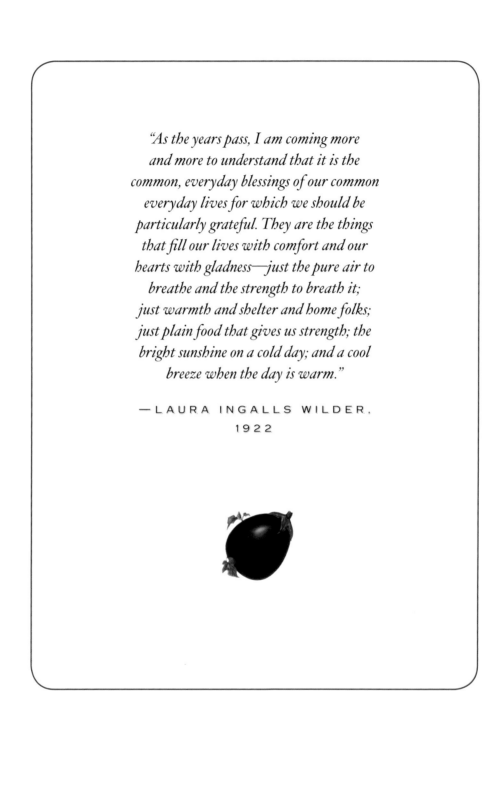

"As the years pass, I am coming more and more to understand that it is the common, everyday blessings of our common everyday lives for which we should be particularly grateful. They are the things that fill our lives with comfort and our hearts with gladness—just the pure air to breathe and the strength to breath it; just warmth and shelter and home folks; just plain food that gives us strength; the bright sunshine on a cold day; and a cool breeze when the day is warm."

—LAURA INGALLS WILDER,
1922

WINTER RECIPES FROM YOUR FAMILY

_____

_____

_____

_____

_____

_____

_____

_____

_____

_____

_____

Acknowledgments

Thank-you to Sandy Gluck, Paulette Tavormina, Paul Grimes, Cindy DiPrima, and the entire team at Rodale for helping bring this book to fruition.

Thank-you to Barbara Melera, the owner of D. Landreth Seed Company, for teaching us so much about what we know of heirloom vegetables and for giving us access to the entire vintage catalog collection from her company. Landreth Seed Company is the oldest seed house in America, and the fourth-oldest corporation of any kind still in business in America. At one point in its history, Landreth sent seed catalogs to every household in America and supplied seeds for the gardens of every president from George Washington to Franklin Delano Roosevelt.

Thank-you to Irwin Richman and the Landis Valley Museum in Lancaster, Pennsylvania, for creating an unparalleled collection of America's agricultural history.

Thank-you to artist Frances Palmer (francespalmerpottery.com) for allowing us to use her beautiful pieces of ceramic to highlight our recipes, to artist Amy Goldman (rareforms.com) for the use of her heirloom vegetables cast in bronze, and for the artists at Christofle.

And thank-you to all of our readers for growing right along with us. Long live Beekman 1802!

Appendix

FINE PURVEYORS
OF HEIRLOOM SEEDS

Baker Creek Heirloom Seed Company: rareseeds.com

D. Landreth Seed Company: landrethseeds.com

Hudson Valley Seed Library: seedlibrary.org

Seed Savers Exchange: seedsavers.org

Seeds of Change: seedsofchange.com

Territorial Seed Company: territorialseed.com

W. Atlee Burpee & Company: burpee.com

Index

Boldfaced page references indicate photographs.

THE HEIRLOOM VEGETABLE STAND
AT THE BEEKMAN 1802 MERCANTILE

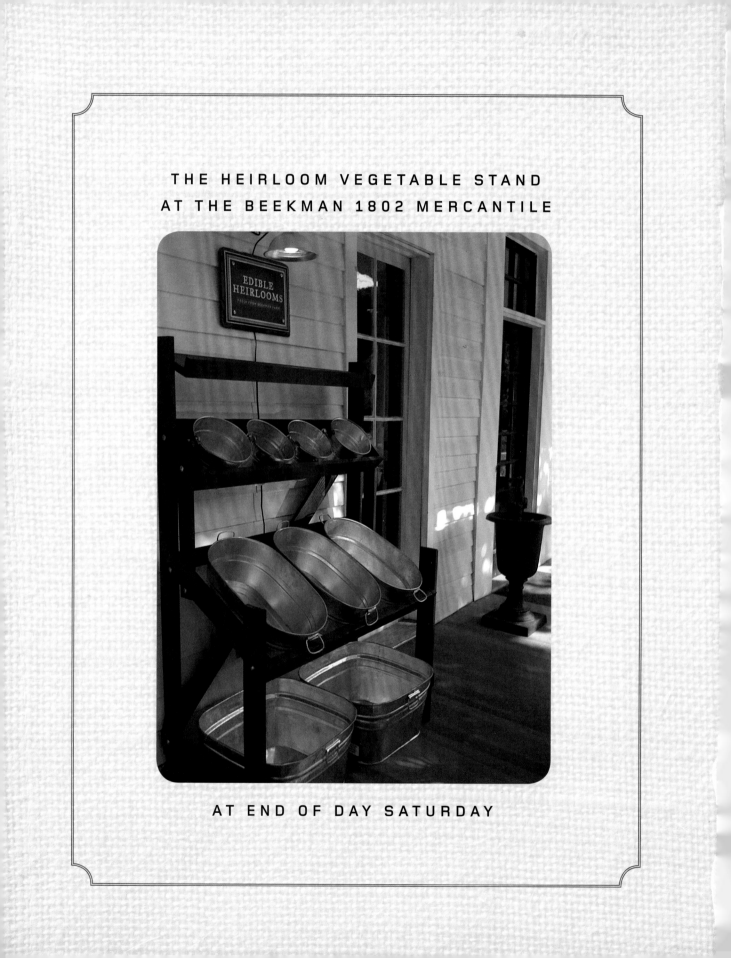

AT END OF DAY SATURDAY

"There's no place like home, except the home garden."

— W. BEEKMAN